CLIMBING
CHAMUNDI HILL

CLIMBING CHAMUNDI HILL

1001 Steps with a Storyteller and a Reluctant Pilgrim

Ariel Glucklich

HarperSanFrancisco
A Division of HarperCollins*Publishers*

FIRST EDITION

Designed by C. Linda Dingler

Library of Congress Cataloging-in-Publication Data
Glucklich, Ariel.
Climbing Chamundi Hill : 1001 steps with a storyteller and a reluctant
  pilgrim / Ariel Glucklich.
p. cm.
ISBN 0–06–050894–9 (cloth)
1. Hindu parables. I. Title.
BL1215.P3G58 2003
294.5'432—dc21   2003049995

03 04 05 06 07 RRD(H) 10 9 8 7 6 5 4 3 2 1

For Jennifer Hansen

Introduction

Mysore's racetrack surprised me in a city of such traditional sensibilities. It was luxurious and lush in a slightly decaying, end-of-the-Raj sort of way. The white paint of the grandstand was peeling and the track surface rarely mowed; the grass seemed tall enough for tiger hunting. A ghostly feel pervaded the place when Rony and I arrived one early afternoon in mid-September 1997. Rony told me that the racetrack doubled as a golf course, which gave the place an eerie, almost surreal feel—despite its ripe beauty.

Mysore was renowned for its Hindu crafts—sandalwood carvings of gods and animals—and for the nearby Sankaracharya monastery, the temples on top of Chamundi Hill, the huge Nandi bull, the centers of Sanskrit learning and yoga, the Hoysala temples, and the Lalita Mahal palace. I did not expect a racetrack, let alone the eighteen-hole golf course that surrounds it, with its last six holes actually inside the track. We found the clubhouse nestled under a canopy of huge tamarind and babul trees, bright with clusters of yellow flowers, just west of the grandstand. Rony insisted on playing every Indian golf course he could find and had inflicted deep humiliation on himself while trying to conquer India's eccentric links.

This one too was lying in wait for the Sanskrit scholar. The tees and fairways were fine, but the greens were not green at all, more like brown or soiled white. A layer of sand covered the hard ground around the flags marking the holes. Players had to putt on a surface where the ball actually left a track and might suddenly stop dead, burrowing into a softer patch of sand. My friend, who relished such strange challenges, booked a round, which included a caddy and a "spotter"—a young boy who would chase the drives and chips and locate every ball, even those that ended up in the waist-high rough. The sun was just past mid-sky, and it was still hot, though a slight breeze was blowing from the direction of Chamundi Hill through the tall thickets of reeds in the wetlands. The area was deathly still, even the crows made no sound at this time of day, and no other golfer was in sight. I knew Rony would take his time, savoring his peaceful obsession unpressed by other players. He asked if I minded giving him the afternoon to play and suggested that I explore the area near Chamundi Hill.

We were not there as tourists. I was recovering from severe illness—sunstroke and food poisoning—which I contracted while working as a biologist in Varanasi. Mysore was renowned for its clinics of Ayurveda with their traditional Hindu healing practices. But, as Rony put it, the papayas alone would cure me. "Let me take you down there," he had said. "It will bring you back to reality." I spent days on the clinic's shady veranda, killing time by watching crows taunt a hawk in the heat of day and butterflies struggle to top a huge coconut tree covered with purple bougainvillea. I loved India during those afternoons—and hated it. My mind was pulled up toward the sky and its promises, but my stomach and muscles kept me stuck in a queasy, swampy place below. After two weeks of treatments I finally felt strong enough to join Rony, who never remained stationary for long.

I took off in the direction of Chamundi Hill. The narrow asphalt road on which we had arrived by motor rickshaw ran from the racetrack toward the wetlands and the dense vegetation beneath the hill. I wanted to observe wildlife or just enjoy the semitropical flora in the half mile between the track and the hill. I hadn't felt this strong in weeks, and I began jogging along the road, then veered off into the marsh behind the third fairway left by the monsoons. I felt a sudden urge to test my stamina against the hill—either that or perhaps the shimmering vegetation drew me to it. The gently sloping four-thousand-foot hill, with its light brown outcrops of granite boulders, reminded me of the pictures I had seen of the mystical Mt. Carmel or a Greek mountain with a temple on top—a miniature Mt. Olympus.

I jogged slowly on a footpath that threaded between the high reeds of the marsh. Dark green water covered with slime and teased by darting insects chilled the breeze as I moved easily. Every now and then the path dissolved into the muck, but I kept going. By the time I emerged at the other end of the marsh, just under the hill, my running shoes were soaked and muddy. Breathing hard, I sat on the step of a small booth shadowed by a huge peepal tree and slowly removed my shoes and socks.

It was a devotional spot—I could see that right away—and therefore hospitably cool despite the hot September sun. Several sacred trees, peepals mostly, spread an immense canopy over the area. Hundreds of pilgrims could fit in that space—Durga Puja, the sacred fall festival for the goddess Durga, must be a riot here—but I was completely alone with a few dozing monkeys. A ceremonial gate led the eye to a stone path, then to four steps made of basalt slab on which pilgrims had smeared vermilion dye in the manner of offerings to a god or goddess. From there the path led between several small booths like the one I was resting in and up the northern face of the mountain. Past the shadowed area of the lower steps the path glistened in the heat.

I began to breathe more easily and felt my strength returning. The steps beckoned. I decided to carry my shoes in hand and climb as far as it took until they dried.

"Just like a pilgrim!"

I turned around just as the old man came out from behind a booth. He was bony and dark, with thick white hair sticking out from under a black woolen ski cap. His brown polyester trousers and green knitted vest over a white shirt defied the heat of the day. He carried a long walking cane, a bag was suspended over one shoulder, and he was smiling broadly as he pointed at my feet.

"You're going up Chamundi with bare feet—are you a seeker? Do you bear a gift of penance for Mahadeva or his beloved Chamundi?"

His English was perfect. I found that rather common in Mysore and throughout South India, but he had startled me so, I remained silent for a few moments, which he took as an invitation to introduce himself.

"P. K. Shivaram, retired librarian for KPTC—that's Karnataka Power Thermal Corporation Ltd., namaskar," he said with hands pressed together in greeting. "How do you do? I don't think it's a very good idea, my friend. Perhaps today you should make do with an offering of marigolds, or just devotion. Your feet," he pointed, "are too soft. Look at mine." He kicked off his cheap rubber thongs. His feet seemed huge for such a small man, flat and cracked and bony like old oars. "Our Shiva is no Jesus, of course, but he will accept even your sweat as a sign of love. Don't kill yourself, young man."

As he talked in his unhurried way, I began to think how silly it would be to tell him that I was merely drying my sneakers, now tied around my neck. It may be dumb to attempt a barefoot climb up Chamundi Hill, but it was more embarrassing to imitate such devout behavior while acting as a porter for wet shoes. So I shrugged and asked if there was any harm in starting up the hill barefoot, then putting on my shoes when my feet began to hurt.

"No harm at all, my friend. Do what you can. I'll tell you what . . ." he added, "I'm going up myself. I do every Thursday—of course, I take the bus down. Would you mind if I joined you, young man?" He did not pause for my answer. "I shall walk beside you if you walk slowly. I am sixty-seven years old, you know . . . Can't go charging up the way I used to when I was your age. But I hope not to slow you down too much."

He was definitely a talker. The words flowed out of his mouth effortlessly, each one chained to the next and inexorably pulling it out. I felt impatient with his chatter and afraid he would slow me down, or worse—discover that I had lied to him about my intentions. But then he surprised me.

"As long as you walk with me, your feet will not hurt—I promise you that!"

I was already at the first step. The stone was warm, even in the shade, and I could feel its rough texture under my soles. "What do you mean? How can you possibly prevent my feet from hurting?"

"Stories, my friend. I shall tell you pilgrimage stories. We have a tradition here. We tell each other stories as we climb up the steps—there are one thousand and one steps, just like the number of Shiva's names. We walk up the mountain telling stories, and the stories have the same spiritual merit as the hardship of walking barefoot up the mountain, or fasting, or chanting the names of Shiva. Some enjoy telling stories because it's an art, while others prefer to listen because of the pleasure that makes them forget the pain. If you pay attention," he paused and added in a conspiring voice, "the stories might turn you into a true pilgrim and give you pleasure at the same time! Let me tell you a story, and we shall see how your feet feel."

I was up at the ninth or tenth step and already the skin of my feet was softening to the rock and warming to the red soil that the rains had washed off the mountain onto the path. Pleasantness would soon give way to discomfort, then to pain, and the old man was insinuating that he could see through me. Clearly the retired librarian was going to either embarrass me or drive me crazy. But before leaving, before putting my shoes back on and running away, I decided to give it a shot.

"Yes, I would love to hear a story. Is it about Shiva or Chamundi Hill?"

"No, not at all. It is about pain, and about the trials of leading a good life while trying to stay healthy."

THE LEPER

Just to the west of this district was a land of luxurious mountain forests. The ruler of that paradise was an avid hunter who favored the more defenseless animals for his game.

One day he spotted a young buck grazing at the

edge of a clearing and raised his weapon for a kill. Just as he was about to release the bowstring, a strange figure appeared between the animal and his arrow. The king lowered the bow and squinted, for what he saw astounded him. He could tell it was a man, possibly old, but so badly misshapen that it was hard to be sure. The man's skin was blotchy with large ulcerous spots, many of them oozing a yellowish-gray fluid, and large flakes were peeling off. His hair was wildly disheveled and dusty, his black teeth protruding through distorted lips. He was naked but for some filthy rags around his bony waist; his emaciated body was crooked like the branch of an old olive tree. As the king lowered his bow, the hideous creature prostrated itself in exaggerated humility.

"I am so sorry for interrupting your hunt, Your Majesty. Please forgive me . . ."

But the king was too bewildered to mind. "Who are you?" he asked. "And what is the matter with you? Are you sick, or are you a demonic spirit? You have the appearance of a ghoul, but your eyes look sad as only human eyes can be."

The man approached, lowering himself further. "I am no demon, sir, but a pathetic mortal here to protect this innocent animal."

"So your interference with the royal hunt was not an accident?" boomed the king in a thunderous, majestic rage. "Don't you know that I am the king and lord of all these lands? Why is this animal worth losing your life for?"

"Your Majesty, I know the forest belongs to you." The man remained low at the king's feet. His voice, surprisingly, gave no evidence of fear. "But I am here to protect you too."

At this the king broke into laughter. "Protect me? What could you possibly mean by that?"

The man hesitated briefly before speaking. "This awful condition that you see, it's leprosy. I did not always look like this." He sank into a sad reverie for a few moments, then continued. "It's a moral disease. You don't just become a leper; it finds you if you commit a sin. With Your Majesty's indulgence, I shall tell you what happened."

The king nodded and dismounted, and the two men sat in the shade of a banyan tree. The leper kept a respectful distance from the king, but immediately began his story.

"Many years ago I owned a farm in the foothills of the magnificent Himalayan range, far to the north. My land bordered on meadows and forests in which a variety of fruit trees and brilliant flowers grew, where bees hummed as they produced nectarlike honey. Into that heavenly wilderness one day my favorite cow wandered, so I went looking for her. For days I searched, but there were too many canyons and ravines in which the dense thicket could hide an entire herd of cows. Despair robbed me of all sense of time and direction—I soon became lost. I grew hungry and tired but kept looking for my precious cow. Then I saw a large tinduka tree rich with ripe fruits growing on the edge of a precipice overlooking a river with majestic waterfalls. It was a frightening place, but I climbed the tree like a fool, looking to reach the ripest fruit at the very end of the overhanging branches. Suddenly the branch to which I was clinging broke, and I fell down, screaming in terror.

"I plunged into the water, reaching the bottom instantly. Fortunately, I managed to push off. The current and fate then swept me onto dry land. I was shivering from the shock and the cold water, but felt lucky to find my body intact. After some time I began to look around for a way to get out, but the place was a trap. The river ran down the canyon, churning through noisy rapids, walled on both sides with sheer rock cliffs. There was no getting out. I saw a few tinduka fruits, which are too sweet by the time they fall from the tree to the ground. Still, I fed on these and drank from the river. In a matter of days—it was obvious—I would be dead. There was no point in yelling, for no traveler would likely come by that remote place. Despondent, I sank to the ground and stayed there, crying and eating the dwindling supply of fruit.

"On the fourth day of my imprisonment there—I was already delirious with despair—I heard a voice from the top of the cliff. 'Who are you down there? Are you man or animal?' I couldn't see the caller, but I cried back as loudly as I could, 'I'm a man. I fell down a few days ago while looking for my cow.'

"'Are you hurt?' the strange raspy voice asked kindly. I managed to focus my eyes on a form above the cliff just under the fruit tree. It was a large black ape with shiny eyes. I hesitated before answering,

'I'm not hurt, but I am in great distress. I fear that I shall die soon.'

"'Don't lose hope,' I heard him say, 'I'll get you out of there. But first let me bring you some nourishment.' The ape disappeared and shortly thereafter a shower of ripe fruit descended on me: bananas, mangoes, and berries. They landed all around, but I ate reluctantly because I was sick of fruit. Meanwhile, the ape disappeared again. He later told me that he went looking for a sack, which he filled with rocks, in order to practice carrying me up the cliff. I thought he had abandoned me, but the next day I awoke to see him climbing down with great skill. It was only when he reached me that I realized how large he was—and how human were his eyes. He told me to get on his back, and I wasted no time. Hanging on to his thick neck as best I could and shutting my eyes tightly, I felt the huge muscles of his back and shoulders as he began to scale the sheer rock. It was a long, difficult climb. With little for him to grasp, the ape often had to suspend himself with only one hand, while his other reached upward to find a new holding spot. His breathing became increasingly strained as the heat of the sun sent rivers of perspiration down his body.

"When we finally made it to the top—as I looked back down, it seemed like a miracle to me—the ape lay down panting on the grass and told me that he desperately needed some rest. 'I must close my eyes for an hour or two. The climb wore me out. After I wake up, I shall lead you out of the forest.' Then he added, 'These woods are dangerous, my friend. There are predators here that will gladly pounce on me as I sleep. I ask you to keep watch for dangerous animals. If I'm attacked and killed, you will surely die as well, so don't fall asleep!'

"I was thrilled to be useful to him. It was the least I could do for the compassionate creature who risked his own life to save a stranger from certain death. I resolved to stay awake and keep a vigilant eye despite my own fatigue. The ape sank into a deep sleep as I sat next to him. The minutes crawled by and turned to hours, while the evening stretched long ahead. Having spent several days in the canyon surviving on a few bites of fruit each day, I was starving for something more substantial than fruit. The thought of eating meat wormed its way into my head and refused to depart. I looked down at the peaceful figure of the ape, lying trustingly on his back with outstretched arms—like a prince on his royal bed. He suddenly took on the appearance of food, a cooked dish. There was so much of him, and I was so hungry . . .

"I knew these thoughts were sinful even as I watched them play inside my head. But the hunger was so raw I couldn't stop. After all, what harm could a thought do? Then it occurred to me that the 'law for times of emergency' would actually allow me to kill my savior! It was an old and revered law. A holy man once ate polluting dog meat citing this law . . . Of course that's complete nonsense, I know it now, but at the time it seemed so persuasive. Before long, I decided to stop my hesitation, this indecisive fantasizing, and I picked up a large stone. I took a good aim at the ape's head and swung down with both arms, already seeing the kill. But then, I don't know, something nudged my hand at the last instant, and I missed. The stone brushed the side of the ape's head inflicting a serious bruise, but failed to kill him. Instead, the animal jumped up and looked around for his attacker. The minute his deep brown eyes met mine he knew. A flash of utter bewilderment passed across his face, and then a profound sadness, such as I had never seen, softened his features.

"'What are you doing, my friend?' he asked in a strangely calm voice.

"His inquisitive eyes were now irresistibly clear, which made me confess on the spot. I told him that I tried to kill him, and I told him why. That made him even sadder, and a few tears appeared in his eyes. 'I cannot imagine the sufferings,' he said, 'that would make you do something so treacherous. Nor can I tell you how sorry I feel to have caused you such a powerful temptation. It must have been impossible to resist—please forgive me.' He spoke with no trace of anger, or even reproach. How could any of this be his fault? His behavior made no sense to me at the time; I just felt shame and a strong desire to disappear, which he must have perceived, for he told me to follow him out of the woods. We walked a long way in silence.

"After some time the ape spoke again. 'I think I understand all of this better now,' he said, 'and I must thank you from the bottom of my heart. You see,' he explained after thinking for a moment, 'after I pulled you out of the canyon I began to feel pride, even some heroic bluster. And you know, our fall begins with mere trifles, but then in no time at all we plunge into a precipice—a moral abyss—deeper than the one that trapped you: egotism. But now you have wiped off every trace of my vain puffery.' He walked silently, then added, 'Unfortunately, you did this at a great cost to yourself. This sin will someday bear grave results. In the meantime, please try to avoid repeating this act, and remember that evil deeds usually begin with a thought.' Shortly after that he showed me to my home and disappeared.

"My life returned to normal. I continued to farm, visit the temple, and donate food to the poor, just as I had always done. The shame of my action never fully disappeared, but it was private shame. Only one other being knew what I had done, and he was far away. Still, that knowledge was enough to gnaw at my soul like a minute parasite.

"Years later, a traveling holy man visited our temple to recite the *Ramayana,* the ancient epic about the righteous king Rama, and to teach us morality. In the evening, before he began his sermon, he told us that everything he knew about *dharma,* about morality and religion, had come from his own master, an ape living in the forests of the Himalayan foothills. The ape, he added, had a deep scar in his forehead, by which we should all recognize him as the Enlightened One, the future savior of humanity.

"That same day—the day my hidden shame became true guilt—I fell ill. Within weeks I reached the pitiable condition you see before you. Even my wife and children shunned me, while strangers turned away in horror at my sight. I left civilization behind, vowing to protect the forest animals from the harm of humans. If I may be presumptuous, Your Majesty, I urge you to avoid the sin of unnecessary killing. I do not expect my disease to be cured in this lifetime, but perhaps my future will not be so bleak. My fondest desire is to die for the sake of a helpless animal."

The king thanked the leper, whom he called a holy man, and returned to his capital. From that day on he forbade all hunting in his forests and lay down his own weapons.

A cloud was covering the sun when the old man finished telling the story, but for some reason I felt hotter than before. My feet were fine, but I felt like sitting down to examine them. We were moving slowly and only made it to the last booth, which was flanked by small nim trees and several fresh-looking tecoma bushes. The old man, who had not looked at me once while narrating the story, now stopped and turned to me with intense curiosity.

"So, my young friend, do you think the king was right to regard him as a saintly man?"

I felt a bit silly being addressed like a pupil by a stranger in a knitted vest on a hot day. Besides, the old eccentric must have known I wanted to look at my feet—he had a bemused little glint in his eye. It was simplest just to answer.

"No, he was merely honest about doing something awful. I don't think that makes him a saint."

"And, of course, a saint would never do something that bad?"

"No decent person would do what he did. Sure, I know saints sometimes claim, maybe even boast, that they are the worst sinners of all. I don't think you can trust them on this. Even St. Teresa, my mother's favorite saint, thought of herself as vile. Anyway, usually they whine about little things— a thought, a whiff of temptation. By their reckoning, everyone is a damned sinner. Their mother sinned just having them. Here it's evident this man did something treacherous. Undeniably despicable."

"Well then, why does the storyteller," he poked his thumb into his chest and winked at me, "bother saying that the king thought him a holy man?"

"I've no idea. You tell me." I was looking around now, trying to find a place to sit, or something to lean on. Would he mind if I sat on the floor of the booth? It looked too decrepit to be sacred. My feet didn't hurt, but there was some irritation there, as though something had stung me.

The old man noticed that I wasn't paying much attention and asked my permission to sit down on the step. Embarrassed, I nodded assent and sat down next to him.

"These empty booths . . ." he gestured with the cane. "In the old days holy men would sit here in meditation or yoga. Pilgrims venerated them like the gods on top of the mountain. Now they're for lovers and old geezers . . ." He looked away when I began to examine the soles of my feet and changed the topic. "Do you think this man was going to heal from his leprosy?"

"I don't really know. I do think you're making a lot out of a simple little story."

"Yes, of course I am. Yes, you're quite right. Please forgive me . . ." For a few moments we sat in silence. There was no sign of a bite on my feet; they were just chafed a bit. Then the old man continued. "You know, we Indians have long since thought that there is a connection between who you are and how you feel. Even the venerable old Ayurveda tells us that the life of the mind and the health of the body are connected."

"Yes, I've heard this often in Varanasi."

"Varanasi? What were you doing there, if I may ask?"

He seemed to have a gift for ignoring my impatient tone of voice, which only forced me to play by his rules. I told him that I was living in Varanasi and working as a biologist. The Ganges, unfortunately, was a fine place to study if you were interested in polluted marine ecology. I'd been there for a year. The old man nodded vigorously, as though we had something in common.

"Ah, the pollution! I see . . . have you found much of it? Our Mother Ganga is said to be ever pure, you know." His accent suddenly became exaggerated, as though he was mocking a foreigner's imitation of Indian accents. His eyes, I suddenly noticed, were a startlingly clear green—like a cat's.

"I'm afraid you've been misled. It's not very pure at all. It's got high levels of chemical pollution, organic, industrial, farm runoff—you name it. Just the sewage . . . You can imagine the health hazard to all those people who go into the river every single day . . ."

The old man broke in, "If I may ask, why did you choose this type work?"

"Lots of reasons. I don't know. I suppose it's intrinsically interesting for a biologist. Maybe it's important. For now I'm just trying to finish my doctoral work in ecological biology—inland marine ecologies."

"But why Varanasi? Why the Ganges? Were you unable to find polluted waterways in America?"

"Touché," I said, feeling irritation travel up my spine. He was nosy and he kept begging for permission to ask, then apologized for asking. I didn't feel like letting him poke around in my life just because he had told me a story. "I'm not sure. I've been to India before, but I wanted to stay a bit longer."

"I understand. With your permission, let's get back to the leper . . . Do you think he might heal?"

"Okay. Sorry." My heart wasn't really in this game, but he was waiting for some answer, so I spoke halfheartedly, academically. "There's a documented connection between psychological facts, say depression, and physical conditions such as infections. But this case, leprosy, is extreme. I mean, you see, leprosy is a disease of . . ."

"Yes, of course," he interrupted again. "What do you think the story is about?"

It was a dramatic shift, but I went right along. "Betrayal. Sin and punishment. Maybe nobility. I have to say, though, it reminds me of one my grandmother's favorite stories. It's a Russian tale, a parable actually, she loved to tell us."

"Would you like to tell it?"

"It's very short, and I'm no good at this. Just a little story about a man who falls into a well and clings to a bush that grows out of the wall. The plant gradually slips out, so he knows his time's getting short. But to make things worse, two mice—black and white—come along and start gnawing at it. That's basically it. I don't remember how it ends. I suppose he falls down. I think it comes from Tolstoy's *Confession*, so he probably does die ... You know those moody Russians."

"Your grandmother was Russian?"

"No, not really. She was from the Ukraine—Kiev. My paternal grandparents came to America when their revolutionary dreams went bust in the late 1920s."

"And how did she, your grandmother, explain the parable to you?" There was that teacher tone again. I decided to ignore it.

"My grandmother replaced her communism with enlightened humanism, then existentialism. She was a depressive. To her the story was about the absurdity of life—you know, a short burst of terror followed by eternal darkness. Just like her marriage, I suppose." I heard a bird call in the trees—a parrot I thought, but I couldn't spot it.

"And you, do you agree with that?"

I did not want to commit myself to a clear-cut answer. He was poking around again and this was too close. "I guess so. Maybe."

"And you think this story I just told you is similar?"

"Well, there's a fall down a cliff followed by a moral breakdown and a punishment, something like that. So I saw some similarity. You don't think so?"

"You're quite astute, for a scientist." He giggled softly. "Of course, you can say a lot about India, but never accuse us of being absurd. My countrymen, you see, do not recognize empty space—a vacuum—precisely the sort of thing your grandmother dreaded. You've seen the walls of the temple at Somnathpur, no? Every square centimeter is accounted for. This one is a story about a world full of things, animals, fruit, intentions, and errors. And every single thing means something. Everything is connected to everything else like the tree vines in that forest in the story."

"So there is no randomness, no accidents or tragedy?"

"Not really. But don't get me wrong, friend. Of course, that does not mean that all's well in our world. On the contrary, things are usually very wrong. Listen to this story." He stood up stiffly, and as I followed him up the steps, he told me the following tale.

⟨ THE BRAHMIN AND THE GOAT ⟩

On the banks of the Godavari, a magnificent river—the very Ganges of the South—a Brahmin was once getting ready to perform a sacrifice for his ancestors. He was a righteous and learned man, jewel of the three Vedas (he has mastered the Vedas and lives by their example), and a magnet for students from as far away as Varanasi. He commanded his students to prepare a goat by taking it down to the river, bathing it, hanging a garland of flowers around its neck, feeding it with grain, and in every other way consecrating it for its ritual beheading.

The students did as they were instructed. They bathed and groomed a large goat, and just as they were ready to garland it, the goat burst out in laughter—a long and ringing laughter, like that of a human being.

"What are you laughing about?" asked the shocked students, but the goat kept laughing. "Tell us what it is, or else the Brahmin will be very angry!"

At those words the goat stopped laughing and began to cry. He moaned and sobbed like a grieving parent and refused to respond to the students' questions. Finally he said, "Take me to your master and ask me in front of him."

The students led the goat to their guru and told him what happened. The man looked at the goat with amazement and asked it why it laughed and why it cried. This time the goat was quick to respond.

"As your students were bathing me and getting me ready for the sacrifice, I suddenly remembered my past lives. I remembered that long ago I had been, just like you, a Brahmin who knew all the Vedas and all its secret rituals. I remembered that one day I performed a sacrifice for my ancestors in which I beheaded a goat. For that one crime I was condemned, through *karma,* to live five hundred lives as a goat, each ending with a beheading. I have now lived all but this one life, and today I shall end the punishment and return to life as a man."

"I am very happy for you, dear goat," said the Brahmin. "But then, why did you cry?"

The goat paused before answering. "I was thinking of you."

A chill ran down the Brahmin's back. He had thought the ritual texts made him safe, but now he realized that if the goat should die, his own fate would be sealed. So he said to the goat, "Do not worry, dear goat. I shall not kill you."

The goat laughed again. "You have already consecrated me. The wheel of karma cannot be stopped. Whether you resolve to kill me or to save me, today I shall die by the force of my own actions."

The Brahmin instructed his students to free the goat, but to watch it carefully to prevent any accident. It was a clear and beautiful day, but as the goat stretched its neck to feed from a bush that grew under a cliff, a thunderbolt suddenly struck a boulder, which crashed down and decapitated the animal.

"So, my friend, can you say why the goat died? Whose karma killed it?"

It was a quick little tale, much less than I expected. We had only covered six or seven steps at the pace he was setting. The sun emerged from behind the cloud, and I squinted as I answered. "To me it looks like his own karma. He even said so himself: 'I shall die by the force of my own actions.'"

"So he did. But isn't it also the goat's karma that causes the Brahmin's downfall? Despite the fact that he tries to protect the goat?"

"Yes, I agree, but that seems so unfair! I mean, if it's the goat's lot to die, why should the Brahmin get entangled in that? Maybe the Brahmin had to work out some of his own karma and at that point in time their karmas—can I even use the plural with that word?—got tangled. Or something like that."

The old man searched his mind for a few moments, then said, "Imagine two cars colliding at an intersection. Four people are injured. How many sets of karma have to operate for such a catastrophe to happen? Could you sort such a thing out?"

His example made me think of medieval theological disputations, and I blurted out, "I don't know, but it's all theory anyway. I mean, that's only one of the things that makes karma so absurd. You don't really believe in this karma business, do you?"

The old man smiled expansively, showing stunningly white teeth. "You're right. Not quite like that. But let's look at it a bit differently. Suppose karma is just a symbol for something. What would that something be? Is it destiny? Morality? Justice? Well, of course it could be all of those. But let's take a risk. Say that regardless of what karma stands for, it always works more like a whole fabric than a single thread. You can't separate one individual destiny from others. Everything you do, no matter how trivial, is connected to what others do and what they experience. You throw away a rusty nail. For one person it might mean a flat tire and a missed appointment, for someone else it may mean a great find—a trade for a rotten banana, a modest meal. When we speak of karma in India, we often mean that people, all beings, are tethered to each other."

"I think that's a scary image. I prefer to think of my destiny as mine alone and, barring any more major accidents, up to me. It may sound cocky, but in some basic way I feel free . . . Oh, and one other thing, if I do something wrong, I expect to be personally accountable; no one else should be." My words came out a bit self-righteously, perhaps too . . . American. I expected a rebuke.

"That's very well put. We Indians are not so fond of this situation either—we call it *samsara*. Everything is tied together in endless interweaving strings of action and counteraction, death, rebirth, and redeath. That's the condition of the world, unfortunately." Off to the west and above us an eagle suddenly dropped like a rock and disappeared around the shoulder of the hill. "And if you think the Brahmin had it bad, you should see what happens in the next story."

THE DEATH SENTENCE

There was a woman called Gautami who lived on the edge of the forest. One day as her son was playing in the woods, he was bitten by a snake and died. A fowler, hearing the woman's cries, came running and captured the snake. He held up the animal, which was squirming and protesting loudly, and spoke.

"Dear madam, this wretched creature is the cause of your son's death. Tell me what to do with it. I can throw it into the fire or cut it to pieces. Personally I'd prefer to burn it alive—it deserves a slow painful death."

"Oh, Arjunaka," the mourning woman replied, "you are completely misguided. Let the serpent go. It does not deserve to die." The fowler was stunned by the bereaved woman's response, but she spoke to him patiently, softly. "You will just be compounding one sin with another. Killing the snake will not bring my boy back to life, and surely the snake can do you no harm. And, not least, this snake has a mother too, who will grieve for him as I do for my dead boy. Would you want to go to hell for causing her grief by killing her beloved son?"

The fowler's confusion now gave way to reproach. "Madam, yours is the view of exceptional individuals, those with a great soul. Most of us are more practical. I know that if the victim were my boy, I would feel a deep satisfaction from revenge. Everyone you ask would tell you that I should kill the snake."

Gautami responded, "No, I don't agree. This kind of grief can't be healed by revenge. Besides, basically good people should try to remain good. The resentment that breeds revenge can only lead to further pain. Only forgiveness reduces pain. And let me assure you that you don't have to be a saint to think this way. At any rate, this may surprise you, but I feel that the death of my boy was predestined."

That last statement, a new twist in the debate, did not catch the fowler off guard, for he responded immediately, brushing it aside. "I beg to differ, madam. This snake is your enemy and killing the enemy is always a good thing. And moreover," he added with passion, "it's not just the matter of your son. This creature will continue to attack others—virtuous animals and people—who count on me for protection."

None of this made any difference. Despite his repeated, sensible appeals, the fowler could not get the mother's permission to execute the snake. She maintained that since her son would not be brought back to life, there was no point in compounding with revenge the violence that killed him. Even the fowler's arguments that gods sometimes kill and that sacrifices can be violent did not sway her. In the meantime, the snake kept trying to interrupt and say something, but every time he opened his mouth, the fowler tightened the noose and choked off his words.

Finally, when the argument reached an impasse, both people looked at the animal, who now sighed and spoke to the fowler. "Arjunaka, you fool. How can you blame me? I'm just a snake! Don't you get it? A snake, a lowly ground-hugging reptile!" He puffed himself up, gathering momentum now that he was allowed to speak. "I don't have a will of my own. I was sent by Death to kill the boy. You may not believe this, but I had no intention of hurting the child, and I certainly felt no anger toward him. It is Death that deserves your condemnation—it is his crime."

The fowler answered angrily, "Why, you pompous little airbag. Don't try to pass on your guilt. Even if you killed the boy at the instigation of Death, you were still the instrument of the killing. Just as sure as the potter's wheel and rod create the pot, you are the cause in the death of this child. You deserve to die!"

But the snake was no mean philosopher, for he exhaled—like the great Shankara in debate—and said, "Ah, the pot and its causes. In order to make the pot, all the causes have to come together. There is no pot with just the wheel or only the rod. And to bring these causes together you must have an intentional will—a plan. If I am just one cause, like either the wheel or the rod, and I have no intention, I can only be innocent." He shook his head in triumphant exclamation and snickered.

The livid fowler looked at Gautami in frustration, but spoke to the snake. "Very well, you may not be the prime cause or even the agent. But you are the immediate cause. It was *your* poison!" He turned to Gautami again. "Let's not lose sight of common sense, madam. It was he who killed the boy. How can anyone possibly deny that?"

"I have to stick to my guns, sir." The snake calmly shrugged what little shoulders he had. "I was merely a bit player here—a secondary cause—not the instigator. And because I have no will of my own, I am innocent. I mean, would you blame the branches of dry trees for spreading a forest fire?"

The fowler turned red with rage. He screamed at the snake. "Words, you're so clever with words. You killed the boy, and I should just kill you now and be done!" The snake was now in immediate danger of dying.

Just then Death himself appeared and placed himself between the fowler and the snake. He seemed pale and smaller than one might expect. Looking at the snake reproachfully, he said, "Snake, it's true that I sent you on this task. But don't keep blaming me!

Neither you nor I are responsible for the death of the child. Just as you were my instrument, I am the instrument of Time. It is Time, not Death, who controls all things. He pushes the clouds around, he mixes the particles of matter, spins the planets and stars, and blows the wind. Time is the mover of all things. You knew this, so why did you blame me for the death of the boy?"

The snake remained unflappable. "I did not mean to blame you, O Death, for this tragedy. I'm only saying that I was sent by you. Whether any blame is yours or not is not my business to pronounce. I'm trying to save myself here." Then he turned to the fowler and added. "You heard Death. He does not deny sending me to kill the boy. You can let me go now."

However, the fowler only dug in his heels more deeply. "I heard Death, yes—fine, but even if he is responsible, that does not absolve you. Both of you are to blame. I curse Death for harming the innocent boy, but I shall kill you for doing the dirty work!"

Now Death spoke again. "Neither one of us is a free agent, fowler. We both depend on Time. It is not proper for you to find fault with us."

The fowler scoffed at this. "That's absurd. If everyone were dependent on Time, as you put it, then there would be no freedom. And if that were true, how would pleasure possibly arise from doing good things, and anger from doing ill? The fact that these emotions do arise is a sign that we are in fact free. Now what do you say to that?"

It was a terrific point that stumped both Death and the snake. Death merely mumbled again that they were both tools in the hands of Time, but he seemed to have lost some conviction. He started to sweat too. At that very moment Time himself arrived on the scene. He turned his grandfatherly head toward Death, then the snake, then the fowler, and finally the grieving mother.

Judiciously clearing his throat, Time spoke. "Dear Arjunaka, you should know that neither Death nor the snake is responsible for the boy's death. For that matter, I am not responsible either. If you want the responsible party here, you must look at karma. The boy was killed due to his own bad karma from a previous life. None of us has any bearing on the store of merit or demerit anyone accumulates. Karma clings to people as light and shadow are related to each other. It's inevitable and tenacious. So there you have it—there is no other cause for this sad case."

The mother nodded, turning to the fowler to second Time's words. "You see? It's all the child's karma. Maybe I also did something bad in the past that contributed, but certainly the snake had nothing to do with that. Now release the snake."

The fowler shook his head sadly. He was completely outnumbered and outranked. He did not like the idea of releasing the snake to bite again merely because of metaphysics. And if karma was a legitimate moral argument, what was he to make of his own violent profession? He laughed bitterly, but released the snake.

The shady area at the foot of the hill was now behind us, and a large granite rock sloped on the right, with a few cactus plants and eucalyptus saplings clinging to the cracks. Heat radiated from the granite onto the path and I found myself standing on the hot soil of the monsoon runoff.

I could not decide whether I admired this story or detested it. It started out with a noble woman showing compassion toward a killer, even making an idealistic case against capital punishment—at least one could look at it this way—but then the story degenerated into a vaudevillian act poking fun at personal accountability. I stared straight ahead, waiting to see if I needed to say anything. The old man, as usual when he finished a story, stopped climbing.

"How do you like the metaphor of the pot and the wheel? I embellished it rather nicely, don't you think?"

I thought his question a bit mischievous, but his green eyes were as clear as a child's. "I'm no philosopher, but if you'll pardon me, I think the metaphor is ridiculous. I'm with the fowler on this one. Assembling a pot out of different elements and deciding to kill someone are in no way similar."

"Because one has a mind while the other is just a material product?"

"Yes, sort of. It's like a machine that will not run if it's missing one part, a piston or a spark plug. All the parts are necessary. With the mind, say the intention to buy groceries, there's just one simple conscious fact. Even if you have no money, or no shop, you still can have the intention."

The old man rubbed his hands together, relishing the conversation. "So cause and effect—chain links such as death, time, karma—these can apply to material things, but not to mind?"

"Yes, roughly speaking, this is so. Even if those three characters—death, time, and karma—meant anything, say, like gravity or alcohol, they still would not be causal. Maybe circumstantial."

"Because intention is simple consciousness and therefore independent of material causes . . ."

"Well, yes."

My guide looked at me with deep interest, as though he had misplaced something in my eyes that he was trying to locate. But he was smiling. "That's a strange sentiment coming from a biologist, no?"

"Maybe. I'm just a marine biologist, an ecologist. I really don't know anything about philosophy of mind. Our fields are so specialized nowadays, you know."

"You mean fragmented? So, even though you are a doctor in biology—yes, almost—what you know about the brain and the mind is no different from what a layperson like me knows?"

"Maybe. But sometimes we have to trust common sense, especially when it comes to consciousness. Only I know what I know, and I know it firsthand. This certainty, the way my thoughts and impressions feel to me, you can't remove it with brain science."

"'I know what I know'—I like that very much. With your permission I shall try to remember to use this in the future . . . But hypothetically, please bear with me, if mind were only matter, then wouldn't it be subject to the laws of matter?"

"Yes, I suppose it would."

"And then we could speak of intention as somehow connected with death, time, karma, or even gravity and beer, no?"

I nodded. He shrugged, then pronounced the entire matter a mystery to him, as though the point of the exercise was just to find out what I thought. The old man pointed up at the rock, "See that spot, under the eucalyptus? It's a favorite place for couples at sunset. Do you have a girlfriend—you're a handsome young man!" The question was more irritating than the hot ground, but he winked and smiled at me. Then he began to walk, and I realized then that until that instant I had not thought about my feet in some time. Then he broke the silence.

"Look, my friend. I know it seems to you that we Indians are trying to avoid personal accountability with this karma and transmigration business . . ."

"You bet," I interrupted.

But he continued calmly, "Let me show you why all of this is sad to us, and why it matters." As we moved slowly, he told me the following story.

THE MINISTER'S DEATH

Quite some distance on a well-traveled road going north used to be a state called Anga, ruled by a young king who was famous for his good looks and great valor. He would have made an excellent king but for one thing. As a young and unmarried man, the king spent most of his energy at the royal harem.

Little was left for administration and government. Fortunately, just as the ancient king of gods, Indra, had Brihaspati to assist him, Yashaketu enjoyed the wisdom and discretion of a great minister, Viveka, a Brahmin whose vision was always clear and expansive. It was the minister who ruled in practice, overseeing the life of a vast domain from a tiny office inside the palace.

One day, rumor reached the ears of Viveka that the citizens of Anga suspected him of coveting the royal throne. Why else, they whispered, would he serve day and night as the de facto ruler, while his master absented himself? It must be some conspiracy! That same day, the minister went home despondently and told his wife about the rumor.

"Why should you worry about rumors and false innuendos?" she asked sensibly.

"Because even a false rumor can hurt the innocent. Look at what happened to Sita when Rama listened to the whispers of his subjects." What happened, she knew, was that the king got rid of her, sent her to the forest forever.

Viveka's wife was a realistic woman who was quick to acknowledge and respond to a genuine problem. She had a ready answer. "Why don't you pack your things and tell the king you are going on pilgrimage to the sacred rivers." This was superb advice, for it would show the city folk that the minister lacked personal ambition and at the same time force the king to perform his duties.

The young king was not very enthusiastic about

the news, and he was still in charge. "You do not have my permission to go on pilgrimage, Viveka." He said. "I need you here and order you to stay!"

That very same night, in pitch dark, the minister bade his wife farewell and slipped out of the city unobserved by the guards or even stray dogs. He traveled simply, like a pilgrim, visiting sacred bathing places in many lands, accumulating great merit. One day he sat down to rest in a Shiva temple in the land of Paundra, near the sea, when a wealthy merchant approached him. The sophisticated merchant, easily recognizing the bearing of a man of distinction, invited the minister to rest at his home. The two men quickly became friends, and a few days later the merchant suggested that his guest join him on a seafaring expedition to the Island of Gold, where he traded cloth for precious metals.

Viveka enjoyed the journey aboard the merchant vessel *Durgatta*. His stay on the island, under a warm sun, passed by lazily. However, on the third day of the return trip, the sails suddenly dropped lifelessly, and the ship came to a standstill. The sea looked as placid as a royal bathing tank at midday, but as a sailor tapped on his shoulder and pointed out to sea, the minister saw that the waves had started to gather up from every direction, amassing into a huge mountain of water that rose up into the sky, dwarfing the ship. The minister stepped back in horror, expecting the wave to crush the ship, but the merchant and the sailors remained perfectly calm. On the crest of the fantastic wave he saw a wishing tree, adorned with gold, coral, and jewels shaped like flowers. Under the tree stood a couch, and on it was a beautiful young woman holding a lyre.

The woman gazed directly into the minister's eyes, picked softly at the strings of her instrument, and began to sing. "Man eats today the fruit he has sown in his previous life. This, even fate cannot change." As soon as the little song ended, the woman on the couch, the tree, and the wave silently returned to the depths of the sea, the water calmly closing in on the apparition.

Viveka excitedly turned to quiz the other passengers. "Did you see that? Have I just seen the most beautiful woman in all of creation, or was it the goddess of auspiciousness, Lakshmi, herself?" But the others merely shrugged—to them the sight he thought miraculous was commonplace. The sailors told him that this fantastic sight materialized nearly every time a ship sailed by, and always vanished after the woman sang her sad song.

The minister suddenly felt overcome with a desire to return home. When the ship docked at port he thanked his host and asked about the shortest route to Anga. It had been months since the day he had vanished, and the king was thrilled to see his weary old friend. "Why did you leave me, good man? This journey of yours was a cruel thing for your mind to conceive, and it did no good for your body either . . . Well, I suppose it was fate, so how can I complain? Tell me, old friend, what did you see on your travels?"

The minister skimmed over the details of his pilgrimages, which he did not expect the king to appreciate, and then proceeded to the description of the sea journey and the huge wave on which the young nymph sang a mysterious song especially for him. "The wave just stopped in mid-flow, higher than your palace, and suddenly a tree appeared in its crest, blinding me with the brilliance of its gems. But above all else, the maiden on the couch was clearly the most beautiful woman in all of existence, although her voice was as sad as the end of youth."

"Tell me more. I want to hear everything!" exclaimed the king in excitement. And, as the minister repeated every detail over and over, the king fell in love in a deep, oddly nostalgic way. When Viveka finished speaking, the king sighed. "If I don't take her for my wife, I shall die—this is certain!"

He ordered the weary minister to take over the affairs of the state yet again because he would soon be departing in search of his love. The minister's protests fell on deaf ears. Yashaketu was already busy disguising himself as an ash-covered, long-haired ascetic, so he could travel without the commotion that usually surrounded a famous king. The very next day he left Anga.

Following the minister's directions, he came upon a hermit called Kushanabha, who recognized the king and told him how to find a ship that would take him to the Island of Gold. The king had to cross three mountain ranges and ford raging rivers, but in time he arrived at the seashore. It was his first glimpse of the sea, which was animated like a living creature, he felt, eager to show him to his destiny's fulfillment. A kind merchant named Lakshmidatta invited him to sail aboard his ship, and they set off for the Island of Gold.

Halfway to the island on a calm sea, the waters rose up again, cresting into a huge wave. The king saw a woman so lovely that he vowed to make her his wife. His love only deepened when their eyes met, and she began to sing her sad song about action, fate, and rebirth.

"Yes," he thought, "she's singing about us! Our love has been ordained by fate. We are destined to be united in love." He extended his hand toward the woman, when suddenly the mountain of water silently sank to the ocean floor. The king was left gazing at mere surface. "She's a nymph!" he exclaimed, then yelling out to the sea, "Protect me and grant me my beloved," he jumped off the side of the ship.

The merchant Lakshmidatta watched the water settle back behind the plunging man. Overcome with sadness and guilt that his guest—an ascetic— had perished, he contemplated throwing himself overboard as well. But then a voice from heaven rang out, "Do not despair, good merchant. The man who jumped into the water was Yashaketu, king of Anga. In a former life he was wed to the nymph who rides the wave—he shall now obtain her hand in marriage again and return to his throne."

And, indeed, the king did not perish. Deep beneath

the ship he kept swimming downward, until he saw the glow of a magnificent city. Marble palaces and temples covered with gold and lined with precious stones stood on the ocean floor, crisscrossed with broad boulevards extended as far as he could see under the deep sea. As he moved closer, searching for his beloved, the king noticed that the city was completely deserted. He entered empty houses and searched in the back alleys, feeling himself surrounded by a gloomy silence. Finally he walked between two rows of formidable pillars into a vast hall of a white marble palace. At the center was a jewel-studded couch, on which lay a figure covered with a green shawl lined with golden embroidery.

The king gently pulled the cloth back, revealing the moonlike glow of the nymph's pure face. She opened her eyes. There was an instant of recognition, before she leaped off the couch and lowered herself at the feet of the royal figure. The king gently raised his beloved, and they exchanged a long glance of deep mutual recognition.

Then they recounted their stories. King Yashaketu learned that his beloved was named Mrigankavati and that she was the daughter of a king who inexplicably exiled her to this desolate place. "I have no idea why he sent me here, and so, every day I rise up to the surface to mourn my fate. It must be some karmic sin for which I am atoning," she told the king with a sad voice.

The king took hold of her hands and offered her consoling words from the bottom of his heart. Then he proposed marriage. "I know we were husband and wife in a previous life. Marry me and I promise to stay with you forever."

"I shall marry you," she answered, "but you must agree to one condition. Four times a month, on the eighth and fourteenth of each fortnight I must leave you for one day. You must let me go then; I promise to return."

The king agreed easily—it was a small price to pay for happiness. The two wed themselves to each other by a mutual declaration of love, in the manner of *gandharvas,* or celestial musicians.

The abandoned city at the floor of the sea was their home, but despite its desolation the two lovers were happy. One day Mrigankavati told her husband that the time had come for her to leave him for the day. "Do not follow me, my darling. I shall be well. And whatever else you do, stay out of the crystal pavilion; it holds a pool that leads to the world of humans. If you fall in there, you shall not be able to return." Having given these instructions, the nymph departed.

However, the king was not content to stay behind. Brandishing a sword, he quietly followed his wife, when suddenly, to his great horror, he saw a huge demon descend swiftly like a nocturnal predator and inhale the woman into the bloody abyss of his mouth. In an instant his wife was gone! The king exploded in a violent rage, roaring like an army of demons. He swung his weapon and decapitated the monster with one blow. Instantly, his rage gave way to mourning as he stepped back and observed the torso where his beloved had perished. But then, before his very eyes, the demon's chest began to move, then tore open from within. Out of his enormous heart emerged Mrigankavati, completely unscathed and miraculously lovely.

The two lovers ran toward each other, but then the nymph stopped and exclaimed, "I remember! I remember everything!" She told the king that she was the daughter of a celestial king who had one day cursed her. "I was away at Shiva's temple worshiping my Lord and lost track of time. By the time I returned, my father was furious. It was then that he cursed me: 'Just as I was swallowed whole by hunger, so will you be swallowed by a demon four times a month!' Then he promised that I shall be freed from this curse, and from my exile, when a king named Yashaketu slew the demon."

The king was thrilled. "Now we can return to my world and live happily among my people," he cried in joy.

"No, my dear. That is not possible. Now that you have freed me from the curse, I am to return to the celestial world where I belong."

"But what about our love? Our marriage?"

The king tried to change her mind, but it was useless. He had been wrong about his fate after all; he was doomed to return alone. But in a flash, a course of action became clear in his mind. He begged his wife to stay with him for one week before returning to her celestial home, and she readily agreed. They spent six days together, drinking from the sweet cup of desperate love. On the seventh day, the king led his wife into the pavilion on some pretext, then embraced her tightly. Before she could fathom his intentions, the king threw himself into the pool, his gateway back to the human world.

A moment later the king and the nymph emerged out of the pool in the palace garden at Anga. Members of the court, servants, and guards came running to greet their ruler, who proudly showed off his new wife. A thunderburst of cheering and clapping of hands accompanied the young couple as they floated into the fabulous palace. The minister heard the commotion and came out of the modest office from which he ruled the kingdom. He lit up in joy at the sight of his master and humbly approached to pay his respects. But suddenly a white pallor descended on Viveka's face. He stopped, and his bearing turned distant and thoughtful. The king failed to observe this as he gleefully displayed the maiden from the wave as his new queen. Viveka, more perceptive than anyone else in the hall, saw that the young woman was shivering with sadness.

"You are indeed the woman from the wave, the celestial nymph." He bowed lightly. "Why do you look so sad?"

"I am sad, wise minister. Because of love I have now lost the power to return to my heavenly home." Her eyes moistened as she spoke.

The king turned in disappointment, but quickly composed himself. "Don't cry, my beloved," he said, smiling happily. He tightened his embrace around her shoulders.

That night the minister returned to his home in silence. Skipping dinner, he went directly to bed, where, a short time later, his wife found him dead of a broken heart.

I had stopped walking before the old man finished the story. Now I suddenly became aware that my feet were turning sensitive; the stone slabs were particularly coarse at this point. Off the path was a cluster of weeds that looked soft, but I only half noted them. The story had almost completely absorbed me.

"Now, my young friend," the old man turned to face me, "why did the minister die? Let us assume for a moment that this story is a riddle. Show me what you can do."

In some strange way I found the death of the minister saddening. It was a good question too, one that went straight to the heart of the story. But I shrugged. "I don't know. There could be lots of reasons, I suppose."

"Such as?" He was beaming.

"Before, when the king was not in love, the minister had to do all the ruling for him. Now, that he's found the love of his life things would likely get even harder for the minister."

The old man clapped his hands and almost squealed in joy. "That's wonderful. What else?"

I studied him closely. There was something disjointed about his reaction: fast and slow, ecstatic and observant, all at once. "Maybe the minister had also fallen in love with the nymph." I suggested. "After all, wasn't he transfixed by the sight of her?"

"Ah yes, that's much better." The librarian turned his gaze toward my feet and remained silent. I looked down too, but there was nothing, just my stupid toes taking turns bearing the load of my feet on the hot ground. "Of course, you're wrong on both counts," he broke the silence. "The minister died because the nymph lost her heavenly home. His own reason for existence thus came to an end. Do you see?"

"In truth, I don't. Sure, she lost her home, but she did end up with the man she had been married to in a previous life. His fate was fulfilled. Isn't that the point?" I had slowly inched my way off the path and was standing in the weeds, smiling sheepishly.

"My friend, if we were sitting on the veranda of the Lalita Mahal sipping on English tea, that would have been the point. Here, on the hill, after the stories I've already told you, the point is different."

"How can it possibly matter where we are?" I sounded edgy.

The old man laughed in a conciliatory way, like a boy. But he said, "As I start to tell you a story, try to keep in mind what we discussed previously. A sitar note at mid-raga sounds entirely different than it does in isolation, don't you think? In this case, we were talking about karma and the transmigration of the soul from one life to another."

"I know." My voice sounded exasperated. "That's precisely what I was saying."

The old man touched me lightly on my elbow, and I felt a soft breeze ruffle my hair. Then he said soothingly, "Did you feel the sadness of the minister?"

Indeed I had. I was moved by his sadness and his death. I nodded again.

"Good, good. That, precisely, is the sadness of samsara—transmigration. The soul journeys from one body to another, from one identity to the next. Do you follow?"

"Are you saying the king is the soul?" The old man was getting ready to chuckle, I could see, so I switched tacks instantly. "No, wait. The nymph . . . the nymph is the soul!" He relaxed now, so I continued. "But how can that be? Isn't the king the hero of the tale, the character in search of a goal? If the soul takes on many bodies over the course of many lifetimes, it is the active agent, like the king in the tale."

The old man began to tap his cane on the stone in rhythm with his words. "He's learning, the boy's learning . . ." Suddenly he stopped and looked at me gravely. "Look, you put your finger precisely on the tragedy of samsara—but in reverse. From where we stand it only seems that the king is the hero. Or, to put it differently, what we regard as our soul—our self, or ultimate identity—that is hardly the soul! In fact the self is the body . . . It's the body, or what Aristotelian theologians called the embodied soul—a false monarch. Do you understand now?"

I did. I really did start to understand him. "Let me get this straight. My soul or what I think is my soul is actually a part of my body and it does not transmigrate, right?"

"That is more or less correct, for now. Our psychological self perishes at death."

"But it—I, the self—thinks it is the soul—the real thing—and so it robs the true soul of its celestial home, its divinity!"

"Brilliant, young man. You are wonderful."

"And that is what makes transmigration sad—this constant falling in love with a false identity . . ."

I turned away from the old man so he would not see my face. I didn't want him to see my excitement. I spotted a datura flower, brilliant yellow, farther off the path and meandered in its direction, feigning botanical interest. In truth, I detested the datura.

Years earlier, when I was fifteen or so, I had conducted a small ethnobotanical experiment with the damn thing. That's a fancy way of saying I just ate some. Somewhere I had read that the datura had "spiritual" properties—it was hallucinogenic. I was not interested in drugs or trips—I think it was just curiosity about how a plant can affect the mind. I don't remember much about the experience. My body became detached from my control and the world slowed down to a standstill. Every moment stretched out to a hellish eternity—there was no pain, only interminable still-ness. I later came to believe that what made that experience so frightening was the psychotic-like loss of selfhood. The body I occupied and the consciousness centered in it did not gel. At a time when I was greedy to be someone, even the most basic self-identity was snatched away chemically for what seemed like an eternity.

My father later said I had been running amok, that my body shook and twitched like a broken windup toy. I woke up in the hospital with tubes running in and out of my body. My parents were arguing, as usual, but I could barely hear my mother. She always whispered when she was angry, which made her more frightening. Mother thought I should be grounded for a year; my father told her to take it easier on me. "Look, honey, he's not a druggie. He's just a budding mystic. Don't be too hard on the boy."

But she was hard. "Mystic, my foot." My mother had curly black hair and savage, brilliant eyes. Her father had been a Jesuit priest who married one of his graduate students at Cal-Tech. Mother, who was a devout Catholic, wielded harsh judgments about religion or about humanity's failures apropos of God. I was grounded for six months. During that time I switched interest from botany to zoology. I loved my father for calling me a mystic.

"You recognize the datura?" The old man was right behind me, looking at the yellow flower. I shrugged. "It is Shiva's plant you know. Better not touch, though, without a guru. Like Shiva, it can be dangerous."

I turned back to the path, avoiding his eyes, and spit out quietly, "Damn right."

Suddenly I remembered a question. "What is the minister then? If the girl is the true soul and the king is the psychological self—the body/mind, I guess—what then is the minister?"

The old man smiled in delight at my question; he seemed positively happy. "Why, my friend, that should be obvious!" he said. "Viveka is wisdom—discriminating intuition. And, of course, he dies over and over again, until we are ready to see the truth."

THE BOY'S SACRIFICE

Not far from here, in the hills to the northwest, is a city called Chitrakuta. It is a jewel of a city, matched in beauty only by the righteousness of its king and the harmony among its many castes. In one of the outlying neighborhoods, a seven-year-old Brahmin boy lived with his parents. The three lived modestly, but the couple felt rich with the joy of having such a special child. The boy, whose name was Thammu, was not only sweet-looking; he was also as mild as a bel tree sapling and indispensable around the house. Above all, he was wise far beyond his years. His parents felt assured that their elder years and their future life would be blessed with security and happiness because of their son's virtues.

One day, as the boy was carrying some firewood to the house, he noticed crowds lining up along the road where a noisy procession of chariots and soldiers was making its way slowly. At the head of the procession rode a dignitary in a high chariot, calling out to the excited crowds. The boy put down the wood and waited for the chariot to come nearer. Finally he was able to hear the strange announcement of that important-looking man: "The king is looking for a seven-year-old Brahmin boy who would agree to offer his life to a Brahmin demon for the sake of the king and the community! The boy's parents will have to hold the boy down, as the king will slay the boy. Anyone who agrees will receive this statue made of gold and gems, along with one hundred villages!" Behind the lead chariot was another in which a brilliant gem-laden golden statue was displayed. It was the size of Thammu and must have been priceless. The crowds were transfixed by the glittering image, but no one seemed to take the words seriously.

The boy had no interest in gold, but, unlike the other merry bystanders, he sensed immediately how desperate the king had to be. With little thought, he

stepped forward and waved to the man in the chariot, the king's chief minister. The official, climbing
down stiffly from the chariot, approached the boy
guardedly. "Yes, my child," he said. "What is it?"

"I want to give my life for the king—I'm seven, you
know," the Brahmin boy said proudly to the stunned
man. "But first, I don't understand why a boy has to
die." The minister, deeply impressed by the boy's dignified demeanor, agreed to tell him about the entire
affair. The two found a shady spot under a tree, and
the minister told the strange account of how the king
came to need such desperate help.

"King Chandravaloka was the worthy ruler of the
renowned city of Chitrakuta. It was he who kept the
castes in peaceful harmony, he who assured the
prosperity of all citizens. But unlike his subjects, the
king remained unhappy because he was unable to
find a woman who would move his heart to love.
And so, the king took out his sorrow on the helpless
animals of the forest, which he hunted with great
ferocity.

"One day as he was rampaging in the woods,
scattering arrows and tearing through a thicket, the
king felt that none of this was filling the void in his
heart. He was overcome with a sudden urge to pen-
etrate the forest to its very core. Striking his horse
with his heel, he sent it flying like a storm through
the green sea and directly into another, hidden
jungle. His companions could not keep up with that
bolt of his horse, and the king was alone. In the
dark new forest his horse slowed down, and

Chandravaloka soon realized that he was lost. He wandered about, more amazed than worried, until he saw a large lake, white with lotus flowers and surrounded with reeds that bent in the gentle breeze, beckoning him to approach and bathe. The king dismounted and cooled down his horse before refreshing himself.

"He was drying off in the reeds when his eyes caught a glimpse of a moving figure. It was a young woman, a hermit's daughter no doubt, for she was dressed in the rough bark of the ashoka tree, with a garland of marigold flowers around her neck. Even the coarse dress and modest adornment could not cover her glowing beauty, the king thought, just as he was struck with the arrows of Kama, the love god. The young woman was accompanied by an older companion—an attendant apparently—who tried to shield her from the stranger's eyes.

"'This must be the lustrous goddess Gauri herself, or perhaps Savitri, the Creator's wife, who came to bathe in the lake,' the king ruminated. 'Perhaps I should ask her attendant.'

"The young woman was too shy to come out from behind her broad companion, but made up for this demureness with thoughts that burned through her mind. "Who is this perfect man who has appeared in this remote forest like the divine King Indra himself? Is he a holy man? He must surely be the most handsome man in the world."

"The attendant, a gifted scholar in the ways of the heart, did not fail to perceive the mutual infatuation,

and she boldly approached the king when he nodded in her direction. He introduced himself as the
king of the land. The attendant in turn, acting on
behalf of her mistress, responded obligingly, 'The
young lady I am shielding behind my back is
Vykunta, sir. She is the daughter of the great sage
Kanva, who lives nearby in a retreat. She has come
to bathe in the lake with her father's permission.'

"The king was thrilled with that information and
immediately mounted his horse and rode to the
retreat, a mere arrow shot away. He dismounted
before entering the compound and approached the
great sage with deference. Touching his head to
Kanva's knees, he introduced himself.

"'I know who you are, King Chandravaloka,' said
the sage, who was a tiny man with an enormous
white mane. 'We all do.' He motioned around him at
the other renouncers who shared the hermitage.
Then he added, 'You are that king who has been ter-
rorizing all the inhabitants of these forests. You are a
fine and righteous king, and you have the best of
everything. Why not enjoy these things and leave
the forest animals in peace?'

"The king bowed low and said, 'Sir, I don't understand my own impulse to shoot animals. I don't really
enjoy watching them die, but the chase fills a void in
my heart. I have heard your words and will abide by
them. From this day on there will be no hunting in
these woods.'

"Kanva spread his arms in delight and hugged the
young king. 'I did not expect you to accept this

feeble request so readily,' he beamed. Then he added, 'Because you have shown such grace, choose a boon and I shall grant it.' The king did not hesitate for a second and asked for Vykunta's hand.

"That very same night, the sacred retreat saw its first marriage, a riotous celebration in which even elderly men of God danced drunk with the joy of the young couple's love. Sadly, the very next morning the couple departed, accompanied to the edge of the hermitage by all the renouncers. From there the two proceeded alone, riding double on the king's horse until dusk. As night drew its lovely curtain of darkness, the king and his wife found themselves on the banks of a deep lake. Nearby grew a dense ashvattha tree, its leafy branches hanging over the soft grass. It was a perfect place to spend the night. The couple lay down on a bed of flowers and held each other as the rising moon dispelled the dark shadows lurking in the creepers of the thick tree. They fell asleep languidly, neglecting to offer the tree any of their curds, sesame, or even water.

"The sun came up fiery and angry. It burned away the last wisps of moon rays and hissed the arrival of a deadly threat. Suddenly, a huge Brahmin demon, named Jvalamukha, hulked above the couple. His hair was flaming like the sun and bright as lightning. Around his neck was a garland of intestines, and he was gnawing on a man's head and drinking the blood from the skull. His protruding tusks were dripping with the blood, and he howled with a frightening laughter. 'Foolish man, even the gods fear this place. Don't you know that this ashvattha tree is my home? I shall tear out your heart and devour it in front of your new wife.'

"The king, who was a fearless warrior, knew he stood no chance against this demon. He looked at his terror-stricken wife and addressed the monster with humility. 'Sir, I beg your forgiveness for this horrible indiscretion. How can I make it up to you? Tell me what you need and I shall provide it, even if it be a human sacrifice.'

"The demon laughed viciously with pleasure and answered, 'Yes, I will forgive you. But only if you obey my instructions in every detail. You must find a seven-year-old Brahmin boy who is of such noble character that he will volunteer to give up his life for you. His parents must hold him down by the arms and feet, and you must slaughter him with your own sword. All of this is to be done in exactly one week. If you fail, I shall devour your entire court. Now go!'

"The king returned to the palace with his young wife feeling worse than he did the day he had left. Everywhere he looked he saw nothing but bloody, demonic death. It was my idea, then, to go around the city in a chariot and make the proclamation you heard and to offer the gold and wealth to the family of the boy who volunteered."

The minister looked at the little boy sitting before him. "I am deeply ashamed for making this request. I never expected a boy to come forward. But now that you have, you must know that the future of our entire kingdom is in your hands." Looking at his hands, the minister fell silent.

The little Brahmin boy was moved by the minister's account. He felt sad for the king, but gave no thought to the gold. With his high and little voice he instructed the minister to reassure the king that everything would turn out well. Then he gathered up the kindling and went to see his parents, who lived in a modest house shaded by gular trees. He told the elderly couple about the king's tragedy and his own intention to sacrifice himself. His parents, of course, refused to hear of it. So he told them about the great wealth they stood to gain from his death, but this only enraged them, and he had to endure a lecture on family values.

When that ended, the seven-year-old spoke the following words: "This body we live in is useless. It is a source of pain and suffering, and it is vile and despicable. In no time it perishes and we die. The only thing that truly matters is the merit that follows us after death, and what better way is there to gain merit than by sacrificing one's life for the sake of others?"

His parents were amazed. "You sound like Lord Krishna, son," said the father. "Where did you get such wisdom?"

"Father, I may be seven now, but my current life is only one in a long chain. My soul is ancient; it has accumulated the lessons of many previous births." The fact that the boy finally talked his parents into consenting was not a testament to their uncaring attitude or their greed. It was a reflection of the little boy's great will and sharp intellect. But finally they did, in fact, agree to let the boy sacrifice himself.

On the assigned day King Chandravaloka took the boy with his parents to the demon's ashvattha tree, where before long the monster appeared, shouting gleefully in true amazement as he beheld the boy. The little boy showed no sign of fear, even when his parents leaned over to hold him down, and even when the king pulled out his sword. In fact, he began to laugh! At first he laughed softly; then his laughter grew uproarious. The king froze in midswing at the very instant that the demon reached out to stop the descent of the sword. The boy's parents stepped back in bewilderment.

"Why are you laughing?" roared the demon. "What can be so funny at a moment like this?"

The boy stopped his laughter and explained. "I can't help thinking how silly this situation must look. Everything is exactly the opposite of how it ought to be. Normally, when a weak person finds himself in a dangerous predicament, he first turns to his mother and father for help. They go to the king, and the king appeals to the presiding deity. Here, all of these persons are present, but they are the very cause of my troubles. The reason I find this funny is that although I'm only seven years old, I can see through the delusions of the body and its desires, while you, who should be wiser, are acting out of complete delusion. You are all slaves to your own body. I think that's funny." And with that the boy continued to laugh.

The old man looked at me with a mischievous grin. "So what do you think—are they going to kill the little boy?"

Frankly I had hoped for some clever twist that would get the boy out of this situation—some of these stories were starting to flatten my expectations. The old man, on the other hand, was another story—the real puzzle. So I shrugged. "Sure, why not? It's up to the demon and he's not going to be moved by the boy's little sermon . . . By the way, can you explain this concept of a demon who is also a Brahmin? I thought Brahmins were always people, and usually virtuous or holy—isn't that the idea?"

"No, not quite. Some Brahmins are people, but some are demons and others are gods. Some are good while others are good by other standards. There are many moralities, you know, just as there are many types of beings and classes of men."

We were standing, and the sun was behind me and to the left. My feet began to burn on the slab step, but I did not want to shift my weight too much. The entire situation suddenly struck me as ridiculous, irritating. This little guy with a happy smile was talking about moral relativism while I was listening like a college student on a field trip, and my feet were turning into sizzling bacon on a hot stove. I tightened my jaw and told him I did not understand.

"Don't be alarmed by that, my friend. In truth, I'm not sure I do either." He looked at my legs and, pausing thoughtfully at my feet, asked, "Tell me, what are your thoughts about the boy?"

The boy? Who cares about the boy! I need to get off this rock! Come on, man . . . "I liked him well enough," I said. "A precocious little thing. Couldn't you make him thirteen though?"

"I suppose I could have, but then he'd be married already and unfit for ritual sacrifice ... It would be redundant, don't you think?" The guide laughed loudly, but showed no sign of moving.

I was beginning to fume and tried to take it out on the story. "I found the argument with his parents too much of a stretch, even if you suspend disbelief. That would never happen with parents who are basically decent, as those folks obviously were. It seems to me that the story is so busy getting out some message that it loses track of common sense."

"That's a very reasonable point, I must agree. So what is that message?"

"Fall in love and you'll have a hungry demon on your hands ... No, I don't really mean that. Look, I need to sit down for a minute. Do you mind?" I turned around and saw a dirt path leading off the steps. A beautiful *Acacia arabica*, with its feathery green foliage, cast modest shade on a comfortable-looking rock. I headed directly for that spot and heard the old man shuffle behind. There was room for both of us, facing the sleepy landscape of Mysore beyond a tall agave cactus that split the panorama in two. This felt good; I picked up the thread of our conversation. "The story's about the end of social morality, I suppose. The protectors stop protecting."

"Yes, and why is our hero a little boy?

"Because he is the ideal scapegoat—the weakest link, the one who needs more protection that anyone else."

"That's very nicely said. The scapegoat. Do you remember the emperor's new clothes, that wonderful story, and the little boy in that tale?"

"Yes, I do. Ah yes, I see what you're saying ... It takes a young child to see through the illusion that everyone else pretends to see—that the emperor is dressed, or that the system is working. That makes sense."

"Precisely. There is a little boy in all of us, a naïve simplicity that is always truthful. It sees through the clutter of moral pretense. It sees through delusion. And, of course, you do not have to be a wise or learned man."

I felt a slight breeze from the west. A few distant clouds framed the lush farmland. "I have to admit that stories about parents killing their children are especially disturbing. I know we have them too—in the Bible, in Grimm's fairy tales. I didn't think I would hear one from you."

"Well, why not?" the old man replied. "There are several. Some are extremely famous. For instance, there's a story about a carpenter who cut a huge green bamboo tree that refused to fall down. It demanded the sacrifice of the carpenter's eldest son. The man agreed and sent the boy with a cart drawn by two bulls, a brown and a black one, to fetch the tree. One of the bulls gave the boy a magical egg and a magical broomstick. At some point the boy began to run away from the tree, which reached out to grab him. So he threw the egg at the tree, and a vicious wind began to blow. Then he threw the broomstick, and a forest of bamboos grew instantaneously. When the green tree crashed through the bamboo forest, it burst into flames, saving the boy. We have stories like that from all over India, but the most important one you will hear only later, when we move farther up the mountain."

"You know, all the stories you've told me up to now are kind of preachy, moralizing . . . but at the same time, there's something passive about them too. I mean, the hero always seems stuck, even when he sees the truth." Just then I noticed that someone had carved two initials on one of the cactus leaves. A ripple quietly tickled my intestines, where I had been so ill, as I continued. "Your heroes have vision but they seem to be moving in molasses . . ."

"I see you need to rest a bit longer. You shouldn't feel ashamed about that. How would you like to hear something altogether different while we sit? Perhaps still a bit preachy, I confess, but certainly not passive."

That was fine with me. I listened as the old man told me the following story.

TOO MANY LOVERS

My grandmother grew up in Varanasi on a rich estate at the point of the river's bend. Her mother was the daughter of aristocratic parents, raised among the wealthiest families—those that socialized with the royal crowd. Her mother's name was Upakosha. From a young age she had been remarkable. She possessed the face of a full moon with lotus-blue eyes, her mouth was framed by coral lips, and her neck displayed the three shell lines of classical beauty. She was a second Lakshmi—the torture of all the young men who ever laid eyes on her. Due to her parents' exalted station, she spent much of her time playing at the royal palace, and in later years studying and performing on musical instruments with the young members of the royal house.

As she approached her twentieth year, her parents felt that it would only be natural if a match were found at the palace, where refined and confident young men of good breeding showed keen interest. However, Upakosha remained extremely modest, keeping strict company with the young ladies. Her studies, which she valued deeply, required that she work with a young man, a tutor who could have bested the great grammarian Panini himself in knowledge of grammar. The tutor, Vararuchi, was ordinary to look at; he could hardly match the court aristocrats in breeding or bearing. Many thought him a fool, however learned he may have been. This was probably due to his awkwardness and lack of worldly experience. It was a great surprise to all, and a savage disappointment to the men of the palace, when Upakosha's parents announced that their daughter would marry the tutor.

The couple lived happily for some time. Vararuchi was the son of merchants, who supplied him with an income sufficient to keep the couple living in comfort. One day he told his wife that, due to the dismal prospects of Sanskrit studies in the region, it became incumbent that he go to the Himalayas in order to propitiate Shiva. He deposited his money with the merchant Hiranyadatta, whom he instructed to honor any withdrawal Upakosha felt necessary to maintain the household.

With her beloved husband gone, Upakosha spent entire days at home. But every morning, as a vow to aid in the scholar's efforts, she went bathing in the Ganges. Although she became pale and thin with her longings, the young woman unknowingly thrilled intrusive eyes as she emerged from her cold bath. Her old suitors had decided to take advantage of Vararuchi's absence and prey on the object of their lust. One day, the prince's minister, a stocky and brutish man, timed his visit to the river perfectly. As soon as Upakosha changed her clothes, he grabbed her arm and forced her toward the reeds by the riverbank. At that moment of crisis, Upakosha proved what an unusual woman she was by staying calm.

"Listen, dear sir," she whispered in her best conspiring tone, "I'd like to rendezvous with you very much. But not here. I mean, there is my reputation to consider, don't you think?" She giggled at him, and he winked back. "Why don't you come to my house next week during the spring festival when everyone will be too drunk to notice. Come at the first watch of the night."

The minister smacked his lips and snorted like a wild boar. "Next week it is, my love. Ah! I have been waiting for this . . ." He released her arm and went away whistling.

It was only after the minister departed that Upakosha allowed herself to feel the severity of the situation. She steeled herself for a solution—there was, after all, more than a week to plan. But then things worsened rapidly. The very next day Upakosha went back to her customary place at the river, where she was accosted again before even entering the water. This time it was the sleazy royal chaplain. He did not assault her—that was not his style—but apparently he had seen her with the minister and threatened to expose her immorality. He demanded sexual favors on the spot. She made the same plans with the chaplain, but told him to come on the second watch of the festival night. The very next day beautiful Upakosha was approached on the street before her own house by the head magistrate. The fat official had an evil gleam in his eyes as he touched the woman in an overly familiar fashion. And so Upakosha had to make the same arrangements one more time, but for the third watch of the night.

She cursed her beauty and her loneliness, vowing now to stay inside, away from the greedy eyes of lechers. That same day she sent one of her maidservants to the merchant Hiranyadatta to withdraw money for presents honoring Brahmins. The girl returned after some time, without the money but with the merchant in tow. The man barged inside, displaying his righteous indignation, and said, "Your husband left no money on deposit, madam. How dare you send that servant to me." Upakosha knew he was lying and merely waited to see what he wanted. And sure enough: "Of course, if madam needs a small loan, I might be able to extend her some credit . . . But I do require something in return." The mistress of the house looked at him coldly; she told him to come the following week, on the fourth watch of the spring festival night.

On the night of the spring festival, the prince's minister arrived as planned, looking as elegant as a hill-station manservant. He was ushered in quietly, his excitement barely contained. However, Upakosha told him that unless he bathed, she would not see him. That seemed exacting but not unreasonable, so he let himself be led off by the maidservants into a pitch-dark back room where he was stripped and given a simple undergarment for his bath. The maids then smeared him from top to bottom with a thick coating of lampblack mixed with fragrant oil, telling him it was a special soap. As they were luxuriously—ever so slowly—rubbing him, the second man, the chaplain, arrived. The minister heard the noise in the front rooms and asked who the guest was. The girls told him that it was a close friend of Vararuchi and an important member of the palace. The minister panicked and begged to be hidden somewhere. It just so happened that a large trunk was conveniently situated nearby, so the naked man was hurriedly ushered inside and told to keep very still.

The chaplain then enjoyed the very same treatment, but before his soaping ended, the magistrate arrived. Then he too was rudely shown into the very same dark trunk with the minister. By the time the merchant was being led into the inner rooms at the last watch of the night, the large trunk hosted three naked members of the royal court. None knew the identity of the others, though all shared a profound desire to escape harm and embarrassment. But the trunk was locked shut.

At the final watch of that romantic night, Upakosha, holding a lamp, led her newest guest—the merchant—to the trunk and said, "Give me the money that my husband has deposited with you for my use."

Seeing that the room was empty the merchant allowed himself to scoff. "Dear lady, I told you that I would give you that money, but only after you satisfy me."

The woman responded strangely. "Listen to the words of the merchant Hiranyadatta, O gods." With those words said, Upakosha put out the lamp and summoned the maids. The merchant was stripped, then covered roughly with the lampblack.

As soon as he was smeared head to foot, the girls shoved him out the door and told him to go home. The man yelled at Upakosha, "You will never get that money now!" However, he slithered home as quietly as a black garden snake, helplessly trying to dodge the dogs that nipped at him. He felt too humiliated to look at his own servants as they scraped and rubbed the sticky lampblack off his entire body.

The next morning Upakosha went to the court of King Nanda, where she was a welcomed guest. She formally accused the merchant of trying to steal her husband's money. The king summoned the merchant, who appeared promptly, barely dried off from his long wash. As he heard the charge, the merchant looked at his accuser with a contemptuous sneer and responded, "I have nothing belonging to that woman."

But Upakosha declared immediately that she had witnesses. "Your Lordship," she said, "when my husband went to perform austerities in the Himalayas, I placed the household deities in a box for safekeeping. They are the witnesses that what I say is true."

The king agreed to have the trunk brought to court, and Upakosha spoke directly to it. "O gods, tell the court exactly what you heard the merchant say. Speak the truth and then go home. Otherwise I shall either open the box in court or set it on fire."

The voices coming from the box were heard very quickly and clearly. "Yes, truly, the merchant admitted that he had the woman's money." The merchant then threw himself at the king's feet, confessing his guilt and begging the clemency of the court.

Of course, King Nanda could not control his curiosity about the trunk, so he asked Upakosha's permission to look inside. She smilingly agreed, and the lock was broken open. Out then came three dark, dazed figures that looked like lumps of coal. Someone yelled suddenly, "Hey look, it's the prince's minister . . . and the chaplain . . . and magistrate!" They were all nearly naked, cowering in embarrassment. The room exploded in laughter and whistling, while fingers pointed at the scrawny black limbs of the distinguished men. Even the king could not restrain himself and screamed in merriment. After the noise subsided, King Nanda asked Upakosha what it all meant, and she told him about the entire affair.

The king summarily ordered that all four men be deprived of their property and exiled. Then, looking admiringly at the young woman, he announced, "This virtuous woman is my sister. Anyone who harasses her in any way is assaulting the very throne." He then sent her home, accompanied by an honor guard.

Now that was more like it. My feet were cooling off, and here was Scheherazade with an old man's voice. I enjoyed not so much the predictable ending as the way the librarian delivered it, playing mischievously with cadence and rhythm.

"I'm glad you liked it," he said, as he waved his walking stick in the air. It was knotty and rough—bilva wood, I thought. "There are quite a few more of these stories, you know, about resourceful women and their suitors, mothers-in-law and other pesky villains."

"Still, I have to confess that I find it a strange story to be telling on a pilgrimage. I'm surprised you told it."

"Why is that?"

"Well, for one thing, it's not religious."

The old man, who was sitting next to me, turned in surprise, as though he had never heard the word "religion" before. He was scratching his chin as he said, "All I promised was to tell you stories that would take your mind off your feet, remember? Did I not keep that promise? And besides, what do you mean by religion? What is a religious story?"

He didn't seem to be philosophizing or setting me up for an intellectual ambush. I felt comfortable telling him that I thought it was obvious. "A religious story would have to be about God, faith, or salvation. And often, telling it would be an act of worship." I was thinking about the scroll of Esther on Purim.

"If you wish, that is precisely what our story is like."

"What do you mean?"

The old man remained quiet for a few moments and stared at the nearby trees. "There are many ways of putting this, I'm afraid," he began apologetically. "To begin with we are on a pilgrimage, are we not?" I tried not to show him my face as I grimaced internally, but thankfully he shifted the direction of his argument. "The way I'd like to understand this story, if you'll bear with me, is this. The woman can be the soul, just like the nymph in 'The Minister's Death.' Her husband would be social morality, the scoundrels are the attachments of the senses to their objects, and the king is the guru. It's a story about learning to renounce sensual attachments as a first step on the path to salvation. All the mischief and low comedy, that's just a way of hiding what is truly going on, or at least saving it for those who wish to see . . . Don't you think?" He looked at me expectantly.

Two things were clear to me. First, the old man did not improvise this interpretation; he had thought of it previously. And second, by the way he was looking at me now, he did not expect his cleverness to impress me at all. Well, I wasn't going to let him down. "If you'll pardon me, sir," I was speaking with the exaggerated politeness of a smart-ass graduate student, "that's a crock of buffalo manure. It's just plain ridiculous. I mean, you're being completely arbitrary— the woman is the soul! Please!"

The old man laughed, in what looked suspiciously like relief. "Of course it's ridiculous, isn't it? The nymph in that other story was clearly a spiritual figure and this woman here is just a . . . heroine. And the story is obviously about lechery because the characters are lecherous. We know it's about ingenuity because the woman is ingenious. The boundary between the obvious meaning and the one I gave is plain and simple, no?"

"Damn right it is."

"Can you then spell out for me just as clearly the exact boundary between what is religious and what is not?"

I started to feel like the cocky chess player who just discovered he had entered a backgammon tournament. But I refused to change course. "I understand what you're getting at, but the story is still not about religion. Maybe it touches a few religious themes—a lot of stories do—but it is not *about* religion properly speaking."

"I can see your mind is made up, and you wish to stick to a distinction you value—I must respect that, of course," he spoke gravely. "But you might look at how you use certain words and concepts when you think, mostly abstract words like 'religion' or 'philosophy.' 'Religion,' my friend, is an empty word—it stands for nothing whatsoever."

That made no sense. Sure, I used concepts such as "religion," or "biology," or "education"—that was true, but so does everyone. That makes them real—the fact that by convention we know what we mean when we say them to each other. I didn't even know what "empty" meant coming from him, so I told him so.

The old man answered slowly. "If you think of religion as some thing bounded and distinct from other things, such as lust or disbelief, then you have no idea what it means to have faith or to engage with God. It is as though you favored studying the sciences of life over living. Since I know that this is not the case with you, I must conclude that

you simply do not trust your intuitions. You let your cate-
gorical mind run your life. And what's worse," he added,
"you're spilling the juice out of a good story."

All of this was too theological for me. I think he noticed
because he suddenly apologized for "getting ahead" of himself, by which he meant, of course, me. I have to admit,
though, that for once I did feel like a pupil.

A sensation that had been pressing under the surface of my
consciousness suddenly floated to the top, and I became
aware that my feet were burning again. The ground temperature was well over ninety. Not as bad as hot sand, of course,
but the effect of the rest was wearing off for some reason and
so was my resistance to the old guide. What had started out
as an ambiguous sensation on the first few steps below and
then developed into heat now felt like a new blister, though I
couldn't find any. The old man was watching with interest as
I inspected my feet for blisters. I was ashamed to let him see
my feet; they were so white and soft next to his cracked leath-
ery soles. There were no blisters, but the skin was sensitive to
the touch—rubbing my hand over the skin felt exquisite. I
sighed, and the old man startled me with a throaty laugh.

"Was that pleasure or pain, that sigh of yours? I think perhaps you should put your shoes back on, my friend. You've
already climbed enough steps to impress Shiva."

"No, I'm fine. It doesn't really hurt."

"Of course not. I can tell your feet are fine, but there
seems to be something else that hurts you, I've no doubt
about it. I can't help noticing that something hurts you.
You're sitting there, rubbing your feet, but you appear to be
enjoying that. Meanwhile—please stop me if you think
I'm intruding—you're constantly shifting your torso. You
straighten your back to a full stretch, then collapse it. You

bend right, then left; then you twist one way and the other. The whole time you grimace and sigh. And what's strangest of all, you don't even seem to notice doing it! Whatever it is—and I'll wager it's your back—you must have had this problem for a very long time."

I only half listened to him. He had a way of voicing his words so you could make out the thoughts without having to pay attention, as though you had just thought what he said on your own. I suddenly realized that my back was killing me, worse than usual. People would notice my discomfort when it got this bad, but I usually managed to draw their attention to something else. I hated the concern, the empathy, but mostly the advice that invariably followed a discussion of my pain. This seemed different though. The old man showed more interest than empathy and was himself so weather-beaten, so scrawny and tough, that I didn't expect the squeamishness that often gave birth to people's empathy. That made me more inclined to talk. I almost wanted to talk. He had been telling me stories in the heat— you could see how hard the breathing came for him. So I told him how my back became such a mess.

It wasn't much of a story anyway. I had been paying for my graduate studies by working for the Bath County electric company, BARC, in the western hills of Virginia. I worked as a climber in a crew that mostly cut right-of-ways for middle-class urban refugees building new homes in the hills. On that particular day in mid-December, the owners of a brand-new little mansion decided to get rid of a huge elm tree that was crowding their kids' playground gizmo: swings, slides, that sort of thing.

We didn't normally do this kind of work, you know, tree service for private homes, but one of the limbs was close enough to the power line that our foreman agreed. The tree might have been dying anyway. We had to get a rope over a branch to control the fall of the tree—so as not to damage that damn swing set. I was one of two climbers on our crew. I wore a leather belt and steel spikes for climbing up the tree and carried a chain saw on a hook on my belt. I would spend most of the day working on the trees. That day the rope got tangled on one of the outer branches, so I crawled out to get it. Bill, the foreman, said I didn't have to, and normally I wouldn't have. But I had just had a mid-morning coffee and doughnut, and my normal bravado was jacked up with a huge sugar and caffeine rush.

Anyway, I don't remember exactly what happened. Most of what I know Bill told me a couple of days later, in the hospital. He said the branch just snapped, and I came crashing down. On the way down—it was a long way, over thirty feet—I hit several branches, which was good because it slowed my fall. Unfortunately, one of those branches cut a huge gash down the right side of my back, ripping the muscles. I landed on the playground set, broke several ribs, and punctured my right lung. There were all kinds of other, minor injuries too. Because of the damage and the scarring, the muscles on both sides of my back were uneven, and there was a constant pull on the spine. Then there was the scar itself, which I couldn't reach. That's what I hated the most—not being able to touch the scar when it burned or itched.

The old man was smiling the whole time I spoke, not a smile of compassion or understanding, like a rookie nurse, but one of a coconspirator. He reacted as though we shared a secret, something that only the two of us could possibly know. But I had no idea what that might have been. I stood up, became aware that I was stretching myself in an exaggerated fashion, and walked back to the path.

"You see," he said, "our tradition insists that all of life is some kind of suffering, like an ache that's always there although we are sometimes too distracted to notice. Even the things that seem right are off center. At some point in life we need to realize this and look directly at the pain. Then we can move to the next stage. May I tell you another story?"

THE BRAHMIN'S QUEST FOR MAGIC

There was once a city in these parts much larger and more glamorous than Mysore. It was called Ujjayini, a glorious town where even Shiva chose to make his residence. The noblemen there lived in palatial estates, while the Brahmins were all learned and modest. Stiffness was seen only in the breasts of the women, fickleness in the rolling of their seductive eyes. The only darkness in Ujjayini was the deep of the night; crookedness was displayed only in the lines of the poets.

In this city of palaces and temples lived a young Brahmin named Chandrasvamin. He was kind and well educated, a member of a prestigious family that had served the city's kings for generations. Chandrasvamin had one weakness, however—gambling. He was enslaved to gaming in all its forms, from taking bets on the weather or the turns in the flight of geese to casting dice in the city's luxurious gambling halls. And like all compulsive gamblers, the renowned Yudhisthira included, Chandrasvamin was both incompetent at gambling and completely blind to that fact.

One day he entered one of the most notorious casinos in town, a dangerous gambling hall where the clatter of rolling dice and the voices of players produced a tumult that challenged even Kubera, the god of wealth, to come try his luck. That nasty sound was completely misread by the tone-deaf ears of Chandrasvamin, who thought—because he was a sucker—that the gods were inviting him to win a fortune against all those other players. He brought plenty of money, and his credit was good too. But before long he lost everything, the beautiful silken shirt off his back included, and gambled himself into a debt he could never repay. The owner of the gambling hall set his thugs on the Brahmin, and they beat him savagely with sticks until Chandrasvamin feigned death.

He remained lying in the corner of the hall for two days, drifting in and out of consciousness, too afraid to move. When the owner realized that the young Brahmin would never pay his debts to the other gamblers, he summoned some of them and suggested they throw the wretch into an empty well; he even promised to make good their earnings. They took him to a nearby forest looking for a well, but an old gambler, out of fatigue or maybe compassion, spoke out. "Look, this man is almost dead. Let's just leave him here to die and tell the casino owner we dumped him in a well. Who would know?" The others agreed and they dropped the body under some bushes.

Hours later the naked Brahmin regained his senses and painfully dragged himself to an abandoned Shiva temple, a small white stone structure deep in vines with thick jungle foliage. Because he was bruised and crusted with dirt and blood, going home was out of the question. He resolved to wait till darkness, then look for food, perhaps even something to wear. Meanwhile he rested on the cool floor. After some time a tall Pashupata ascetic looking like Shiva himself walked into the temple. He had long matted hair, and his nearly naked body was smeared with white ash. In his right hand he was carrying a long trident. The holy man recoiled at the sight of the broken Brahmin, but hurried to offer him help. Chandrasvamin, lowering his eyes in reverence for the holy man, introduced himself softly. Despite his obvious shame, he told his story honestly, without covering up his own fault.

The ascetic smiled compassionately and said, "You have suffered too much for such a minor sin. But it was good fortune that has led you into my hermitage, for I shall help you heal and feed you until you feel ready to go home." He offered some rice from his begging bowl, but the young man declined.

"Thank you, sir, but I can't eat that food. As a Brahmin, I am permitted to eat only food cooked by other Brahmins."

The ascetic apologized for his absent-mindedness and told the Brahmin not to worry. He possessed a magical power, which he now called forth, commanding it to nourish the Brahmin.

At that very instant Chandrasvamin found himself in a golden city, sitting under a mango tree in a luxurious garden of jasmine, roses, vasanti, and fragrant henna, dressed in silk garments with golden embroidery. Seven female attendants, all lovely and sensual, floated like mist out of a marble pavilion and beckoned him to rise and enter. The most beautiful among them took his hand—he could smell her soft water-lily perfume as she led him to a throne inside the house, where she made him sit beside her. The attendants brought tray after tray of heavenly food beginning with fruit: sliced papaya and pitted mango, guavas and bananas, sweet oranges and sugarcane. Then came the main course of flavored boiled rices, vegetable savories, pancakes made of wild figs cooked in clarified butter, and sweetmeats, which his beautiful companion fed to him with her own hand. He finished the sumptuous meal with betel nut flavored with five fruits. The meal made him drowsy, and he fell asleep reclining on satin pillows, with a soft hand stroking his head.

He woke up in the morning to the sounds of the forest, lying on the floor of the old temple. The ascetic was there, staring at him with a kind, inquisitive smile. "How was your night, good sir?"

The Brahmin was feeling a grave loss. "I enjoyed the night, sir, but without that beautiful woman my life will be empty. I must go back to that garden!"

"Yes, I understand," said the renouncer. "As long as you remain my guest you shall be able to visit your beloved. My science will transport you to bliss again and again."

This arrangement worked for a while, but finally the young man lost patience with having to rely on the power of another man for his own pleasure. He begged the ascetic to teach him the secret of his wondrous power, but met only refusal. "This science," he heard, "is far too difficult to acquire, especially for someone as young and inexperienced as you."

But the Brahmin persisted. "Why?" he asked. "What makes it so hard to learn?"

And so the ascetic explained. "The science of creating new realities can be mastered only while you sit at the bottom of a river, chanting a secret spell. The science will erect obstacles to confuse you."

"What kind of obstacles?"

"I can't really say—it's different for different people. You might be frightened by demons and ghouls, while someone else could be lured by beautiful sirens. Some may experience themselves as strangers: young or old, foolish or wise, a man or a woman. Perhaps even a she-wolf. But regardless of what the magic does to you, at a very specific time you will be summoned by the power of your instructor in a very subtle way: it will dawn on you that your experience—your life and identity—is an illusion. You will then have to climb a funeral pyre and burn yourself, without hesitation or fear, and walk out of the river in which you have been sitting. Should you fail to do so, you will never see your beloved, and I too shall lose this power forever. This is why I hesitate to teach you the science—I fear your inexperience."

But Chandrasvamin refused to listen. Driven by his desire for the beautiful woman of his visions, he pressed the holy man daily, until he broke down the resistance of the sage. That morning, the two men went to the river, where the ascetic showed the Brahmin how to enter the river and where to sit. He gave him the spell along with instructions. "Repeat this charm in the water, and you will immediately encounter the power of its magic. Meanwhile, I shall be right here on the bank. I will summon you when the time is right. Do not hesitate to respond to my call!" The Brahmin followed his directions precisely.

Just then, in a nearby district, a child was born to a family of the carpenter caste. He was a beautiful and passionate baby, a bawler with an insatiable appetite for his mother's breast, a responsive giggler to the adoring attentions of all the women in the extended family. He grew up to be a spoiled but sweet child, nurtured by everyone who knew him until he became a soft and lazy young man. He passed the time in daydreaming, playing pranks on his relatives, or wandering the fields and hills of the district. Even his father shrugged off the young man's slack disposition. When the time came to find him a wife, the parents scoured the surrounding districts for an appropriate social match who would be beautiful and generous, someone who would cheerfully take care of their boy. They found a fair-complexioned girl with long limbs and sparkling eyes, a distant cousin from another carpenter family. Her patience and kindness domesticated the young man, who finally began to learn carpentry and gradually help around his father's shop.

As the years passed by quickly the young couple gave birth to a boy and a girl, whose growth only made time accelerate further. On the day that the carpenter's son turned twenty-four, his oldest—the boy—was already six and almost ready for school. At midday, when the carpenter's son walked home from the shop, a vague recollection percolated into his consciousness. He stopped and closed his eyes. It was something like déjà vu—but stronger: another reality, images from other places (familiar places, but he had never been anywhere!), a voice. Suddenly, unaware of how he came to know this, the young man was sure that he had to end his life, burn himself on a funeral pyre. He remembered—or felt—someone who had told him to do this. Was it a dream he had? From a previous life? But he was sure now; he knew what he had to do.

Everyone thought this was another hoax—his worst joke yet. As he spent the afternoon building the woodpile, friends and relatives gathered around, half of them joking, the others gesturing impatiently, waving away the joke. But for the first time in his life the young man acted decisively with steady hands preparing the pyre for lighting. That was when the family members realized he was serious, and pandemonium broke out. His wife and his mother ran at him and grabbed his shirt. Shrieking, they tried to pull him away, while the two children, who were confused and horrified by the women's hysteria, started to scream for their daddy. His father was seen lecturing at him, but no words came out, or perhaps they were drowned by the noise of all the people there who were yelling at him or crying. The carpenter's son looked at his little boy, the very image of his own distant childhood. His heart seized in his chest—and he hesitated. Will the boy take care of the women? Will he miss his father? He turned to the little girl and ran over to hug her. But the voice exploded in his ear, and he finally tore himself away and lit the wood.

Something stunning then happened. The roaring flames that burst from the dry wood—pushing everyone back several steps—the fire that consumed him as he climbed his own funeral pyre was as cold as snow. It had felt hot from the ground—but now, sitting on the pile, he was shivering cold. He opened his eyes in surprise and found himself at the bottom of a river. Suddenly he remembered and shot up to the surface. On the bank of the river, standing quietly, was the Pashupata ascetic, looking like a figure from the distant past.

Chandrasvamin walked out of the water, shook off the memory of his family along with the water in his hair, and then lowered his head in respectful salute. He did not know how long the holy man had been waiting there. Twenty-four years—that was the duration of his life as a carpenter—seemed too long even for such a great sage.

As though reading his mind, the ascetic said, "You were under the water for as long as it took you to speak the spell twice. That is all. Now tell me, what did you experience?"

Chadrasvamin told him everything that took place, ending with the mysterious cold fire. The ascetic was somber. "Son, I'm afraid you made a mistake, either with the spell or in some other detail. The flames have to be hot. The cold flames punctured the mental reality."

"No, sir. I'm sure I used the correct spell," the Brahmin cried, and to prove it he repeated the words accurately.

"Still, something went wrong. You will not have the magical power, and I probably lost mine as well." The holy man tried to call forth his science, but nothing happened.

The Brahmin repeated his story and began to cry, feeling that he had lost his beloved forever. But then he remembered his dear wife, whom he also loved, and his Brahmin father, and his voice became faint and unsure. "What did I do wrong? I did exactly what you told me!"

The holy man looked at his student sadly and

said, "You hesitated. You clung to your life, refused to leave your wife and children." He added, "It was a brief hesitation, just a few moments, but the chance was even briefer, and it went by forever."

We were stopped under a *Ficus bengalis* that looked like it was dying—it was a perfect hangman's tree with its naked limbs running parallel to the ground. The old man leaned against the tree. He looked at me expectantly, waiting perhaps for a compliment or a question.

"So that's it?" I asked. "It's now back to his miserable old life of gambling and losing?"

"I don't know, really. The story just ends there. What do you think of it, my friend?"

I suddenly remembered my feet, or else the sensation crossed a threshold again, because I began to feel a burn. I found a shady spot under a low scrubby tree and sat on a rock. The bottoms of my feet, which I had totally forgotten for a while, were bright red, like lobsters in boiling water. The soil added to the raw color, but when I tried to brush it, the redness grew deeper. I muttered a curse, and the old man laughed. Of course, he was wearing his thongs.

"So now you're really feeling your feet I see. It's my great story that made you forget, don't you think?"

He seemed serious about that, so I scornfully said, "I find it very ironic that a man of god, a man of Shiva of all gods, would use his great powers in order to help a compulsive gambler achieve his sensual—his sexual—desires. That's the reason he lost his magic. The whole thing is so amoral, it's beyond me."

At this the old man laughed out loud and made a few rapid comments about my puritanical sensibilities. But then he said, "No, my friend, what the Pashupata taught our hero has little to do with wealth or women. It's about time, or better yet, about timing. He gave him another life in the blink of an eyelash and showed him firsthand how easy it is to miss one's chance."

"Chance for what?"

"Chance to wake up to what is real. To see through *maya*—the cosmic illusion. It's like that pain in your feet. They have been burning for a while, but you have felt nothing. Your mind was elsewhere. Suddenly you woke up to what was there all along. It makes you wonder, doesn't it? What are we missing all the time that is constantly here? What kind of voice does it take to wake us up from the dream of our life? A good guru can teach us these things, but who can find one? And besides," he added as he turned and poked his finger lightly at my chest, "who wants to wake up from this dream?"

We continued the climb. I resolved to keep my shoes off for a while longer, but only out of pride and stubbornness. "It seems hopeless then," I said. "You miss your one chance, which is too easy to do. I mean, how do you tell a true voice from a false one anyway? And then you're stuck until you die, or forever maybe." I was now moving gingerly, planning carefully where to plant each step. "A one-shot deal. You blink and you lose. I really don't see the point of trying."

The old man was watching my deliberate walk and said, "No, not once. That's your Western tragedy, not ours. We try again and again, if not in this instant, then the next, or if not in this life, there will be another, or the one following that. The opportunity is always there, although the key is not to look for external signs, but to realize that the issue is perception itself. Let me tell you another story."

THE TURTLE BOY

A long distance to the south of us, on an island I believe, a king and his chief minister made a very unusual arrangement. They vowed that as soon as they produced offspring, they would have them marry each other. Regardless of who had the son and who gave birth to the daughter, their children would surely marry.

As the years passed the king was far luckier than the minister in progeny. Though both worshiped the amalak tree according to the tradition for obtaining sons and both prayed to Shiva often, the royal couple gave birth to several daughters, all lovely and clever. Meanwhile, the minister and his wife were able to give birth to one male child only, and a turtle at that. The minister's wife was pregnant with Turtle Boy, as he later became known, while the queen was carrying her first girl, and so the two were promised to each other. Of course, the royal couple was mortified to discover the identity of the match for their eldest, whom everyone regarded as the most beautiful girl in the land.

But a deal was a deal. When Turtle Boy reached a marriageable age, his father went to the king and announced that the time had come for uniting the two families. The king tried to change the topic for a while, commenting on the weather and the latest palace gossip. Finally he coughed, cleared his throat, and said, "You know, my friend, these are modern times. Why not let the children decide whom they wish to marry. Let us go and ask my daughter. As she decides, so shall it be." The minister, who was in no position to argue, mumbled his assent, and they went to the young lady.

The charming princess, radiant like a reflecting pool in a mountain garden, found it inconceivable that she should marry the turtle boy, but she knew her father was in a bind. So she agreed on one condition. "I shall marry him," she said gravely, "providing he can bring me the solar-love flower." The king smiled to himself. How could any mortal obtain that flower, about which even gods have only heard rumors? Turtle Boy had no chance. Downcast, the minister returned to his son and told him of the new condition for marrying the princess. The turtle, however, was not discouraged at all. "I can do it, father," he exclaimed enthusiastically. He ignored his father's doubts and set off, lumbering slowly on his four legs, in the direction of the rising Sun.

It took the turtle a long time to reach the east, the place where the Sun rises every morning in his flaming chariot. When he finally arrived at that place, exhausted and famished from the long journey, Turtle Boy did not delay at all in executing his plan. Just in front of a huge arka tree, which would conceal him from the rising Sun, he lay down his shell across the path of the chariot and stuck out a fifth of his body. He hoped either to be crushed by the chariot wheel or win an audience with the Lord of Light.

The Sun, indeed, stopped the chariot in time and addressed the turtle lying in his path.

"What are you doing there my boy? I nearly ran over your head!"

"I beg your pardon, Lord Sun," answered the turtle. "I did not mean to delay your journey. But my life is worthless unless I get one-fifth of the brilliance of your rays."

"And why, son, do you want all that brilliance?"

The turtle told the Sun about the princess and his impossible task. He explained that being brilliant would undoubtedly lead to great things—to the rare flower itself. The Sun nodded compassionately. "I shall give you the fifth part of my rays' brilliance, but you must come out entirely from that shell." As soon as the turtle crawled out of his shell, a blinding ray of light struck him and he became a fair-skinned and handsome man.

"There you are, my child. Your soft self is now revealed to the world." The Sun gloated over his handiwork. "But now we must get you that special flower, the solar-love flower. I've heard of it, but have never seen it. I must admit I like the name ... Unfortunately, the only one who knows how to get this flower is a godling who sleeps for a month at a time. In order to get to him you must first go through the godling who sleeps for two months at a time, and the road to him leads through the one who sleeps for three months at a time. Make sure you are there when they awake, and they will give you what you need." With these strange instructions the Sun left the minister's son, who retreated back into his shell and went looking for the godlings.

Following the Sun's instructions closely, he was able to obtain a magical gift from each of the three godlings: a deadly club to beat the demon that ruled the forest, a flute that could summon anyone and make any thought manifest, and a bag for obtaining whatever one wished. Finally, the last godling sent the turtle to a lake in the heart of a distant forest. There the turtle hid behind the reeds, carefully observing the advice he had been given. As noon gave way to evening and the light softened, three virgins appeared, dressed in beautiful rainbow-colored saris. The three young women quickly disrobed and jumped into the water, sending soft ripples that rocked the blue lotus flowers. When the women were deep in the lake, the turtle came out of the reeds and scooped up the pile of their clothing. The virgins shrieked in dismay, but he took off as quickly as he could and disappeared into a temple that stood a few steps from the lake. Then he locked himself behind a large stone door.

Soon he heard tentative footsteps behind the door and then a knock. "Mr. Turtle," they spoke as one, "please let us have our clothes back. We shall give you anything you desire."

"Can you give me the solar-love flower?" he asked skeptically.

"Yes, we can. Just give us our clothes, and we shall go and fetch the flower for you."

But the turtle was no fool. "No, that's not a good idea. Here is one sari. The one who gets dressed can go and get the flower while the others wait."

That set off a chorus of protests as the young women struggled to cover their naked bodies. "Please don't make us wait here naked, sir," they begged. "The shame is too much to bear."

"Well then, you may all go, but you must first take an oath that you will bring me the flower."

The virgins swore solemnly and got their clothes back through a half-opened door. They dressed hurriedly and ran to fetch the flower. It was a tiny flower with yellow and orange petals that smelled like the dawn. As Turtle Boy reached for it, they quickly stepped back. "What are you doing? You promised me the flower!" he cried.

The oldest-looking of the three said, "We shall give you the flower, there is no doubt about that, but you must first answer a simple question. Which one of us is the most delicate?"

The boy did not lose his patience; he was intrigued by this riddle, but asked how he was to judge such a thing.

The oldest spoke again. "Once on the way to the pool I walked under a pear tree and a single blossom petal fell on my head. I fainted on the spot and could be revived days later only through the diligent work of the royal doctors."

The second virgin then spoke. "One summer night I slept on the roof of our house, and a light breeze blew my nightshirt off my arm. A single ray of moonlight hit me, and I was crushed. Only the best physicians were able to revive me and restore my health."

The third virgin spoke last. "Some time ago I was lying on the bank of the lake and drying myself in the breeze. Several miles away a woman was pounding grain with a pestle in her kitchen. Immediately painful blisters appeared on my body, and I became severely ill."

Turtle Boy was impressed and congratulated all three for being the pinnacle of delicacy. Then he pronounced the youngest as the most delicate. "The youngest is the only one who made no physical contact with the object of her torment. The flower and the moonbeam, though fine, did in fact touch your bodies. The sound is truly distant, and therefore only the most delicate girl would feel it." The virgins said nothing, but gave him the flower.

The minister's son returned home quickly in his human form, but crawled back into the turtle shell as soon as he arrived. He asked his father to lead him to the palace, where the king was mortified to see the modest-looking solar-love flower. He cleared his throat repeatedly and shuffled his feet, waiting for some miracle to intervene. In contrast, the princess was true to her word and happily agreed to marry Turtle Boy, who had managed to obtain for her that rarest of all flowers. She even smiled at the turtle with true affection. The wedding was a grand affair because at that very same time the king scheduled six other weddings for his other daughters. The six lovely girls had been matched up with eligible princes, and the six handsome unions completely overshadowed the wedding of the oldest and most beautiful princess and her embarrassing husband.

After the seven honeymoons passed by in the blink of an eye, the king decided that it was time to select a successor to his throne. Because the king had no male issue, the heir apparent would be the man who could pass a simple test. Each of the young men, dressed in white clothes and riding a white horse, would hunt in the forest for six days. Whoever could kill and bring back the most impressive game would be declared the winner.

Six husbands armed themselves and confidently mounted their magnificent horses. They disappeared in six clouds of dust in the direction of the forest. The turtle received neither horse nor weapon. His wife, the king's oldest and dearest daughter, actually had to beg for an old mare and a short sword that could not cut through a ripe papaya. He was hauled on top of the pathetic beast and, to avoid falling off, his wife tied him down with some zucchini vines from the garden.

As soon as he disappeared into the forest, the turtle slipped out of his shell and landed on the ground as the handsome prince that he was. Using his magic flute and bag, he obtained a white horse and white silken clothes and then, with a mere thought, commanded all the forest animals to assemble before him. They were led by the demon who ruled the woods, but the prince dispatched him with a quick blow of the club. He stood waiting, surrounded by thousands of large and small beasts in a vast clearing and, as he had expected, the six princes eventually arrived.

When they saw the majestic figure with all the animals surrounding him they exclaimed, "Greetings, Your Majesty. You must be lord of this forest. We have scoured the woods from one end to the other and have failed to see a single game animal. And here they all are with you!"

"What is your wish with my subjects?" asked the prince.

The hunters told him about the test they were facing and begged for permission to hunt. The prince shook his head, but said, "I shall give you each a deer if you lend me a piece of your clothing." The six men gladly accepted the strange offer and tore off pieces of fabric from their royal shirts. Then they rode back to the palace to show their game. The prince, meanwhile, retreated into the shell and told his wife to present the king with the better half of a rat. The king was as furious with this offering as he was delighted with the six large deer. In a fit of rage, he drove the princess out of the palace.

In the course of the next five days this very same routine repeated itself, but the young men had to offer other articles to the turtle prince in exchange for their game: rings, earrings, locks of their hair, and other items. It was a small price to pay for the chance to become heir apparent, and the king was properly impressed with all of them.

On the final day, the turtle made preparations to go before the king in order to make his own case. When the princes saw him lumbering in his shell, they burst out in laughter and joked that his chances would improve if he were to bathe or anoint his shell. The turtle ignored their nasty comments and went off seeking privacy by a pond. He removed his shell, in which he kept his three magical objects, and entered the water. Unbeknownst to him, his wife had seen him emerging from the shell and was struck by his beauty. As her husband swam in the lake, the princess seized the shell and threw it into a pot of boiling water. The prince emerged out of the water into his wife's arms, his shell gone forever. He dressed in blue and gold silk garments, and the two went to the palace to meet with the king.

"Who are you?" asked the bewildered king when he saw his daughter walking next to a striking young man.

"I am Turtle Boy, the minister's son and your eldest daughter's husband," the prince announced. After a pause he added, "And I am the heir apparent."

At these words everyone in the room burst out in laughter. After all, he had been able to procure only six half-rats while the others served up deer and antelope and boasted great hunting skills.

"Your Majesty," said the prince calmly, "at the cost of interrupting all this merriment, I must tell you that it was I who captured all those animals. I gave them to my brothers-in-law in exchange for these." He tossed on the floor all the things he had collected from the princes—pieces of clothing, earrings, locks of hair—and told the king about the bargain he had struck with the six men.

The king glared at the princes with barely contained rage. "You lied to me," he boomed, "deceived me like a dumb tourist in a flea market—just to win the throne!" He promptly demoted the six to the status of court servants and gave all his daughters to the turtle boy, whom he pronounced heir apparent to the throne.

We had moved only a few steps from "hangman's tree," I realized, but I was happy for the old man's slow pace. "What a strange story! I really don't know what to make of it. It reminds me of 'The Frog Prince,' I suppose."

"Ah yes, the golden ball in the pond . . . And here we have a solar-love flower—what a wonderful coincidence. And what do you make of the frog prince, then?"

"I don't really know—as a marine biologist I'm highly skeptical . . ." The guide laughed kindly at this. "It seems like it's about coming of age, learning to accept sexual feelings. I'm not sure—there's something very psychological about it."

"And our little turtle boy here, is he also coming of age?"

"Possibly. Coming to terms with who he really is, his inner nature—the prince, I guess."

The old man pointed behind me to a smallish tree. "Sandalwood. This is our staple here in Mysore—have you bought any carvings?"

The sweet-smelling figurines, hand-carved with great care

to avoid any sign of individual artistry, were everywhere in the city. I loved their smell and had picked up several broken icons that had been left on the floors of workshops— that made them unique and eccentric. I shook my head.

The old man asked, "Was it wise to tell this story when I did, after the Brahmin's failed magic?"

I could not fathom where he was going—it was one of those questions he liked to ask in order to set me up for a theoretical point. Or so I thought. "I'm not sure, but there seems to be some progress there. The Brahmin failed, he remained stuck, while the prince learned how to move forward."

"Toward something?"

"Sure. He seemed to be more fully adult, confident. He became more authentic to his inner, true self—damn, it sounds so corny when I say it."

"Well, don't torture yourself about it. It's an excellent answer. Of course, it's exactly the opposite of what the story is telling us, but that's another matter."

I knew it! I knew there was something I should have seen, but didn't. I'm not sure what it is about old Indian men, guides especially. They have a gift for making you feel like a child, and the harder you fight that feeling, the worse it gets. But I was curious. "What do you mean?"

"From where I stand, it's a story about having a very solid sense of self, a rigid one in fact. And it's a story about getting rid of that notion, attaining selflessness, transcendence. That is what the kingdom stands for, you know." He winked mischievously, which seemed to undermine what he was saying, but he continued. "It's a gradual process, my friend. We can't achieve transcendence immediately. We must first win the princess—that's immanence, it's the *atman* of the Upanishads. You've heard of these scriptures, I'm sure. And to win atman—of course, we've never lost it—we must first obtain the solar-love flower . . ."

I had read the Upanishads, as Rony urged me to. My friend also explained some of the famous passages, about Yajnavalkya and Janaka, and Shvetaketu and Uddalaka Aruni. I learned about the individual self merging with universal Self, but I doubt I understood it any better than Emerson and Thoreau had two hundred years earlier. Still, I thought I knew something. "Don't tell me," I pleaded with the old man, who was just watching me. "The flower is the grace of God!"

"That's very nice," he smiled. "I like that, although that's not what I was going to say."

Of course not. What did I expect? "What then?"

"Perhaps I should not say, you're giving such wonderful interpretations. Who knows, perhaps you're right and I'm wrong. I should not like to lead you astray . . ."

"But what were you going to say about the flower?" I raised my voice. "I'd like to hear . . ." He could have been teasing me, but there was no way I was going to let him change the topic. "Come on, oblige me!"

"Let me just say that many of these stories—especially about animal people—are about who we are in our ordinary existence, how we come to be the people we are, and how to unmake all of that. The essential first step—renunciation—means untangling our ego, our very identity. Although the goal is transcendental, the means are always mundane. We control them, not God."

"So the flower is some psychological symbol, not a divine one?"

He shook his head and smiled at the same time. "As you

might expect, I do not like these distinctions. Let's just say that the flower is a key in the process of unmaking who we have come to be through our family's expectations or those of our friends—our place in the world. For each one of us such a key exists, but it is unique."

"Well then, why is it solar, and a flower?"

The old man began to laugh. He rolled his head backward and grabbed his sides as he roared, but there was no malice in his laughter. He seemed happy for some reason—perhaps he liked my insistent focus on the flower. "The reason it's solar and a flower is because it's my gift to you. It's your key, my friend, and no one else's. Remember that." After he settled down a bit, the guide added, "I know this is hard—let me help you with another story."

Just before he began we heard an excited voice behind us. Several steps down the path a man about my age and a boy were bending over a step and gesturing excitedly. We backtracked immediately—I suspected a snake—but when we reached the spot, the source of excitement turned out to be a small common tree frog. The tiny amphibian had been shading itself next to the step, but the sudden commotion made it panic. It tried to hop up to the next step, but failed repeatedly. The boy and his father—I assumed they were related—argued about something and laughed. I asked the librarian to translate.

"The boy wants to take the frog home, but his father claims that the frog is a pilgrim and must not be disturbed." The man, who was wearing green trousers and a cotton shirt, appeared modern enough—a professional man. Was he teasing the boy or was he serious? The boy seemed more excited than disappointed. Suddenly, the frog, which had gathered some strength, took several quick leaps sideways and disappeared behind the green tecoma shrubs. The father and the boy stared at the spot, then noticed my feet. That made them forget the frog—they giggled happily. In an instant they turned around and charged up the hill.

TO TRUST A WOMAN

The gentleman who was my neighbor before I retired, a successful merchant named Udhay, once told me this story about his days as a young man. He told me that he had been the only child of a couple who suffered through a tense marriage. His father was a wealthy trader who had married an exceptionally beautiful woman—just because he thought it would showcase his earnings to competitors. Unfortunately, she may have been too beautiful for him, and he never learned to trust her. Even when she was pregnant with Udhay, their only son, he suspected her of infidelity. It was not until the boy was born, showing a crescent birthmark on his chest—identical to his father's—that the merchant relinquished his suspicions about the pregnancy.

The rich merchant loved his son and spent hours playing with the boy or sharing the wisdom he had accumulated in a fruitful life. He taught him how to be assertive around other boys, how to make and invest money, but mostly how to conduct himself around women. Long before the boy was ten, his father already lectured him about the dangers of feminine wiles. "Be careful with women, son. Especially the pretty ones. They will lead you on, make you think that they love you—but in truth they are always planning your downfall." Little Udhay did not get much out of these lectures; his father was very disappointed to see the boy run to his mother and ask her what daddy was talking about.

The boy loved his mother. She confined herself to the house, managing the household and the servants, often telling him stories, and showing him how to worship the gods. He sensed his mother's deep sadness, although her demeanor would suddenly become overly joyful whenever her husband came home. To the boy this meant that his mother was trying to cheer up old Lemon-Face.

As Udhay grew into a teenager, his father assumed an even more active role in educating him about the ways of the world. He brought him to work in his shop, occasionally even on business trips. Once, when the boy was fifteen, his father took him to the district capital on a trading expedition. At the end of a long workday, the merchant showed Udhay to a famous brothel in order to demonstrate to him just how cunning and dangerous women can be.

The madam of the house was a monstrous old woman called Yamajivha. She had a huge protruding jaw and crooked teeth beneath a bulbous nose. She shrieked in laughter at the sight of the sweet-looking boy and his serious father. "Wait here," she said rudely to the two guests, "I'm in the middle of something."

Then she turned to her daughter, who was hardly more attractive than her mother, and said, "So you hear what I'm telling you? Men are worth only as much as the size of their wallet. The ones with money—even if they are old and ugly like this one with the kid—you must love. Those who are penniless— even if they look like Kama himself—throw them out. Do you understand?" The girl nodded vigorously, as though trying to make up for an earlier mistake.

The old wench then turned back to her guests and rubbed her hands. "What can I do for you gentlemen today?" She eyed the boy with relish, but the merchant stepped in front of his son.

He pulled ten gold pieces out of his pocket and handed them over to Yamajivha. "My dear madam, you have already taught my boy everything he needs to know about love. I hope this is enough reward for the lesson." He took the boy's hand and led him out.

The old prostitute ran to the alley and called after them, "Come back anytime, master, there's plenty more wisdom where that came from." Then she walked back in and slammed the door.

By the time Udhay turned sixteen, he was begging his father to let him go out and earn his own fortune. Over his wife's protests the merchant agreed, but he gave his son a large sum of money to get him started. As a concession to his wife, the merchant agreed to select a companion for the boy—Udhay's paternal cousin Arthadatta, who was two years older. The young men set out at the head of a caravan, along the river in the direction of the sea. In a few days they reached Kanchanapuram, a ramshackle town of river traders where even morality was up for sale. They camped some distance outside of town, intending to continue on the very next day.

However, that evening the two young men dressed in fine silken clothes and went to see a dance at a local temple. Udhay made eye contact with one of the dancers—the most glamorous woman he had seen in his young life. The dancer, Sundari, smiled at him sweetly, and Udhay immediately told his companion to return to the caravan and unpack for a long stay.

"I think I'm in love, dear cousin," he said grandly, as a wealthy teenager might.

"I don't think this is a good idea," Arthadatta pleaded. "Why don't we leave right away?" But he left the mesmerized boy at the temple and returned to camp.

Udhay had never been in love, but he always imagined that love would have to be won. Some of his favorite stories were about separated lovers or infatuated heroes having to pass a test or conquer a shy princess. This was thrillingly different. After the performance Sundari simply came over and touched the young man's feet in respect. He introduced himself to the girl, who, blushing, invited him to meet her mother.

The two women lived in a well-appointed house—the foot-washing bowl Sundari's mother brought out was covered with gems. The older woman, Makarakati, was dignified with quick and sharp eyes—like those of a hawk—that seemed to take everything in. The young man found her intimidating, but her devotion to Sundari was obvious, especially when she hugged her daughter and said, "He's such a handsome young man, and obviously from a respectable family. Be nice to him, my dear!" That made Sundari blush again, and Udhay felt his own cheeks flush. They lounged on silk pillows all evening long, feeding each other fruit and sweets from crystal bowls, which were served by two discreet maidservants. Every now and then when Udhay felt his hostess accidentally brush against his arm or thigh, he recoiled in pleasure. He waited for some signal that he should leave, but it never came.

Late the following morning, Arthadatta saw his young cousin entering camp, floating like a sleepwalker. "Where were you, young cousin? We were all so worried about you!"

Udhay took that as reproach and snapped out of his reverie. "Don't father me, Arthadatta. I spent the night with my beloved." His face softened with the sound of that word. "Now, where is the chest? I need to withdraw some money."

"What for?" Asked the cousin.

"I need to make a small loan to my beautiful Sundari; it's just a temporary matter. Where is it?"

"Well, how much do you need?"

"It's not your money and not your concern. But if you must know—one million."

Arthadatta was appalled. A million bought you a stable full of the best horses, with food for a lifetime and an army of stable boys. It was nearly one-quarter of the boy's total wealth. "Listen, boy, don't you recognize a scam? You're walking straight into it with your eyes open and your pocket bleeding dinars!"

These words deeply offended Udhay. "It was my idea to give her the money . . . She refused to accept it."

"So what happened?"

"Her mother persuaded her . . . sensibly, I thought. She said that because we were lovers, we should be sharing everything, and that Sundari might as well accept my offer."

"You're a damn fool, cousin. And don't forget, it's not your money either—your father gave it to you."

But Arthadatta was wasting his breath. The young man took the money and disappeared again. The trading expedition dissolved into a long, idle wait by the river, while the infatuated young merchant spent most of his time at Sundari's house. Two months went by, and half of Udhay's money found its way to his lover.

One day Arthadatta was angry enough to confront his cousin with harsh words. "Listen, cousin, you're completely out of your mind. That girl, Sundari, she's just a dancer—a performer. Do you have any idea what that means?" He got no response and continued. "She's a prostitute, man, a whore. She's had other men and now she's out to rob you. Wake up!"

But even this brutal honesty had no effect on Udhay. "I know she's a dancer, but she's not like the other ones. She's pure and beautiful, like my mother. You and everyone in father's family are just jealous of beautiful women, but I'm not. Besides, she loves me with all her heart—I can feel it."

"What you feel is not love, cousin. Trust me."

Then Arthadatta had an idea. "Look, I'll prove it to you. Let me come with you to Sundari's house and just suggest that we should leave. She'll drop you on the spot."

The young man agreed, and in the presence of Sundari and her mother Arthadatta executed his plan. "Ladies, I'm sad to tell you this, but Udhay and I have spent our fortune and must now resume our business journey." Looking at Sundari, he said, "Your beloved will only grow richer, and he will certainly return to you when the time is right." He then paused to observe the reaction.

Sundari looked devastated. She began to shake and sob silently, allowing herself to be enfolded within her mother's arms. Then she turned to Udhay and said in a pitiful manner, "You're abandoning me for the sake of wealth. I was no more than a station on your journey. Oh, my fate . . . I gave you my heart . . ." she sobbed uncontrollably.

But her mother calmed her. "Don't cry, my dear. I'm sure he will return. You must let him go now."

Arthadatta led his cousin out by the arm. "You were wrong—she doesn't want me to go!" cried the youngster.

But his cousin said, "Let's just keep this going a bit longer. We'll lead the animals away from town and see what she does."

The next morning Udhay's group prepared early and took the western road out of town, walking slowly toward the coast. Just then Sundari came running from the city, calling out for her beloved in despair, her hair blowing wildly. As the men turned to look at her, she suddenly threw herself into a well. Udhay reacted quickly, but before he could reach her, three shepherds who happened to be near the well scampered down and gingerly carried out the injured woman, whose clothes were in tatters.

The merchant was beside himself with guilt. Gathering Sundari into his arms, he begged forgiveness, tearfully promising that he would never leave her again. It was a joyful moment for the two lovers, whose great passion burst into flames, fueled by tears and fanned by remorse. Standing off to the side, Arthadatta watched glumly.

Udhay, now emboldened by conviction, moved into his lover's home; he was hardly ever seen at the camp. Once a week he came to collect clean clothes and more money, then disappeared into his sweetheart's bejeweled bed with its silk canopy. He spent another two months of renewed sensual joy, until one day he returned to his cousin with ripped clothes, bruises all over his body, and a bewildered look on his face.

"What happened, cousin?" asked Arthadatta.

Udhay was too embarrassed or confused to speak. He stared down at his shoeless feet and remained silent.

"She threw you out didn't she? She threw you out! What happened—did you tell her you ran out of money?"

"Well, I did run out of money, but so what? What does that have to do with anything? I thought she loved me . . . She threw herself into a well for me!"

"Cousin, I have let you down, and I failed your father too. Not only have I not protected your money, I've been unable to teach you even a modicum of common sense. Come on, we're going back." Within hours, the caravan was assembled and turned back upstream.

Back at home Udhay's father was furious. "I'm very disappointed, son. Didn't I warn you about women? Did you forget what the old whore Yamajivha said? Women are mercenaries, boy, all of them!" Udhay turned to look at his mother, but she was too meek to say anything. He was in no position to argue either, having lost almost five million of his father's dinars. "Come on, son, we're going back for more instruction," his father barked. By the time the merchant's wife finally spoke up, protesting that the boy needed some rest, the two were already out the door.

Yamajivha was also furious, but only at herself, and she showed it by laughing and swatting her daughter's head. "She threw herself into the well," she roared. "That's one of the oldest tricks in the book. I should have warned you about some of these tricks." She turned and slapped her daughter again. "Okay, gentlemen, you can have your money back, or you can have my daughter. Which will it be?"

That made her laugh, and the two men looked at each other blankly. Their silence made the old woman shriek "Ala!" Then again, "Ala!" Suddenly a monkey jumped in through the rear window and scampered onto the old woman's shoulder. "Gentlemen, meet Ala. She's my gold-making animal. You can have her for a few weeks—she will get your money back."

"How will she do that?" asked the merchant.

"Just feed her twenty gold pieces every morning, and she will do the rest."

The merchant looked at her suspiciously. He was entirely predisposed to suspect the old prostitute of a scam, but this was his town—he knew where to send his friends in the police department if he had to. His son, meanwhile, seemed lost—it was not clear at all that he wanted his money back. On the way home the merchant warned Udhay, "Listen, son, I don't know what you're thinking—that girl did not love you; she just wanted your money. You may not believe me, but you will obey. You will take this monkey back to Kanchanapuram and win the money back. It's not negotiable!"

The young man put on his best clothes and left with a small group, including Arthadatta. The monkey was allowed to sit in the saddle with him. He arrived at Sundari's house looking fresh and eager, and he was greeted earnestly if not warmly. "How nice to see you, my dear young man," said Sundari's mother, who was the one who ordered him kicked out as soon as he had admitted to running out of money.

Now Sundari came and put her arms around her princely former lover and intoned, "Have you come back to show me your love? I'm so sorry my mother was upset with you."

Udhay stammered and appeared uncertain as he announced that he was sure of Sundari's love and that he had returned to reclaim it.

"Well then, to celebrate you must buy me a lovely meal in the finest restaurant!" She clapped her hands excitedly.

Before the young man could answer, Ala jumped in through the window, climbed up onto Udhay's shoulder, and spit out three large gold pieces.

The two women could not believe their eyes. Sundari, who was as quick as her mother, immediately spoke again, "And, of course, I shall need a new dress." The monkey spit out two more gold pieces. "And some jewelry." Four gold pieces came flying out.

Udhay was treated like royalty again, and the next morning he returned to his friends' camp. There he fed the monkey twenty gold pieces and returned to Sundari. They spent the day together, but when the young man saw his beloved flirt endlessly with the monkey, he finally realized that he had only imagined his perfect love. Eventually, Sundari offered to buy the monkey for thousands of dinars, and Udhay refused. Then she offered half her wealth, but he still refused. It was the first time in his young life that Udhay had conducted a business transaction, and he was rather pleased with himself.

The following morning, Arthadatta, who was

thrilled by the recent developments, suggested that they feed the monkey three days worth of gold, and the animal gorged itself on sixty pieces. When Sundari and her mother begged to buy the animal in exchange for their entire fortune, including the money they had hoodwinked out of Udhay, he finally consented and left the monkey in their possession, along with these instructions: "You must let Ala roam about freely. She will spit out the gold only when you make a request." To demonstrate he asked for two gold pieces, and the monkey obliged.

The caravan departed, loaded with a huge amount of wealth, its young leader finally liberated of his false notions of love. Back in town the two women rejoiced over their gold-making creature and greedily demanded more and more bits of gold. After two days, when Ala had spit out all there was, the women flew into a violent rage—they realized they'd been conned. They attacked poor Ala, but she scampered off and disappeared into the woods. Weeks later she showed up at her old mistress's house hungry but happy.

The old guide stopped walking and turned to look at me. He seemed very happy with the way he told this story, a major achievement considering that one could see the story's end halfway through.

"So what have you learned from this cautionary little tale, my young friend? Would you rather trust a woman or a monkey?" He tapped the bilva cane on the stone in soft rhythm till I spoke.

"If the story is any guidance, I'd go with the animal. Is that what the story's really about? I mean, you've been digging beneath the surface of all your stories."

He nodded in agreement and said, "Why don't you tell me? You're probably getting the knack for this kind of thing."

Well, why not? I thought the meaning of the story was obvious, even if you didn't take the gold and the mercenary sex literally.

I could not be sure how many steps we'd climbed—the view below was magnificent. The path reached a right-handed dogleg, and a large crimson rose butterfly floated gently in the direction of the sitting spot I was aiming for. The librarian reached out his cane easily, and sure enough, the dark butterfly came to rest on it. I took that as an invitation to sit too.

"I think you could say that men's wealth represents our better aspirations, maybe spiritual goals. Women have the effect of distracting a man, or draining his spiritual energy, through sensuality and comforts. In the previous story you said that a man must learn how to give up his place in the world. Well, I suppose women represent a huge obstacle to that. I mean, don't renouncers have to give up sexuality? I know Buddhist and Christian monks obey vows of celibacy above everything else."

As I spoke the guide watched the butterfly, though he seemed pleased with what I was saying. At the end I thought he was ready to applaud. Instead, he just wiped some sweat off his face and said, "I can't speak for Buddhism or Christianity. As far as P. K. Shivaram is concerned, this is misogynistic nonsense."

"Okay, okay," I jumped in defensively. "I don't mean that the women themselves are obstacles—that they're intrinsically bad. I mean that a man's attachment to women is what holds him back, the same as his attachment to other things, like cars or fame."

"That's a decent recovery, young man, but we could do better."

"How then?"

"Let's take the story as a parable about the different layers of experience. For instance, the relation between fiction and reality, dreams and waking experience, imagination and memory. Do you follow this?"

"Absolutely not!"

"Did you notice the relationships between the boy and his mother, the ugly old whore, and the pretty Sundari? The boy was particularly attached to his loving and beautiful mother, which made him construct an imaginary perfection out of Sundari. The stark realism of the ugly woman—and her lesson—was completely invisible to him. The imaginary worlds we create around us are projections of what we already know, the mother, and what we already know comes from those things that satisfy our basic survival needs. Isn't that what mothering is all about? So the mother is the satisfying emotional reality, the whore is physical reality in its brute and unadorned form, and Sundari is the fantasy or fiction we create by projecting one type of reality onto the other, which we repress. In other words, the women in the story don't stand for things in the world; they stand for different types of worlds. Are you following this?"

He made sense, I had to admit, at least as far as the theoretical consistency of what he was saying. It didn't seem to match the story closely at all, but I was starting to get used to the fact that he picked and chose his way through anything that suited him in these stories. "What does the monkey stand for?" I asked.

"Good question, my friend. The monkey is that principle one uses to reverse the illusion he has created out of his experiences. It has to be an animal—the opposite of the humans who engage in world building. It gives back only what you put into it, and although it can deceive, it never does so with prejudice—it only deceives those who are predisposed to deception because they fail to see that it is a mere animal. If you're good to it, it will be good. If you're nasty, it can bite or in some cases sting you with poison.

"In short, the monkey stands for storytelling. What we are doing right now on this mountain is what the monkey represents in the story in relation to Udhay. Restoring a sense of balance—insight—to a world in which fiction and reality have become hopelessly mixed, where we fail to realize that what we see is conditioned by what we know."

"But why a monkey? Why not a dog or a cow?"

"Well, did you see the monkeys at the bottom of the hill?"

Come to think of it, I did see a few bonnet macaques dozing on the roof of a booth. They were well fed and contented—unlike the aggressive, flea-bitten variety I was used to fighting in Varanasi. I smiled and nodded.

"They have to be monkeys because monkeys are in-between creatures. They are part animal, part human; they walk on the ground or jump in the trees. And monkeys are also mischievous—they jump this way and that; they hurl things at you to get your attention. That's what storytelling does."

"So this story is just about literary interpretation and not about religious or mystical ideas at all?"

The old man feigned anger by sticking out his chin and furrowing his brow, then said in a deep voice, "I shall not dignify this kind of question with an answer. Come, look at this graffiti."

FATE OR CURSE?

My grandfather's servant Gotama carried himself like a nobleman. He was not a lowly servant, mind you, like those who cleaned the house or fixed things; he was more of a personal assistant. Still, he acted like the equal of any aristocrat, and my grandfather did not seem to mind. On business travels or hunting expeditions Gotama would oversee the preparations and check on the stable boys and the packing. Once the journey was under way, he often rode alongside grandfather, and the two of them would talk for hours.

Grandfather was a nobleman, a minister in the king's court and a proud man. He respected Gotama's self-esteem and often relied on the older man's wisdom. One day as they were riding together, grandfather asked his assistant how he came to be so self-assured.

Gotama casually answered that his confidence should hardly surprise anyone, considering his royal ancestry. What was surprising, he told his listener, was that he ever came to be a servant in the first place.

Grandfather, who normally observed the privacy of his servants, could not control his curiosity and immediately asked, "What act of fate or karma led you to your present station? Was it a terrible sin one of your ancestors committed?"

Gotama responded defensively that it was neither fate nor karma, but the result of a curse. He then told my father the following story.

The last man in Gotama's ancestral line to actually serve as a king was Maundibha Udanyu, king of a prosperous and peaceful state. In his kingdom lived a Brahmin called Yavakri, who was the worst scoundrel who had ever lived in the country. Yavakri was a privileged and overindulgent young man with a lethal power that very few Brahmins possessed and fewer yet would ever consider using. This power allowed him to seduce women with one magical sound: "Hay!" Any woman who heard him produce that sound felt immediately compelled to sleep with the monster, only to die as soon as he was satisfied. If by some miraculous strength of will she was able to resist the urge to sleep with Yavakri, she died sooner.

One day, when King Maundibha was performing the prestigious and rare horse sacrifice, this despicable Brahmin came to watch—waiting for a chance to cause some mischief. Moments after the priests uttered the first ritual chant, Yavakri interrupted. "Ha! You made a mistake! I knew you would, you imbeciles ... You chose the wrong verses and now," he turned to the pale king and poked his finger in the air, "you'll be dead in one month, Your Royal Majesty."

The king was no fool. Although he feared the curse of the excited Brahmin, he did not feel powerless. Immediately he instructed the priests to destroy all the implements used in that unlucky ritual and to smear the royal houses with mud. "This expiation," he explained, "will protect me. And let it also be a pledge." He turned to Yavakri. "It is you, Brahmin, who will die. And as soon as you die, I will return to my sacrifice and complete it according to the law."

Yavakri was amused by the king's little drama. What were the king's chances against the curse of a Brahmin? He turned away contemptuously and headed back into town looking to inflict pain on someone else. His chance came sooner than expected, and in the person of the king's own cousin, Mamsi. Poor Mamsi happened to be heading toward the king's ritual grounds just as Yavakri was leaving, and one look at her full figure and pure chocolate complexion made that dreaded sound echo in the alley: "Hay!"

The young woman turned her head in the direction of the voice and knew her fate in a flash. It felt like a burning itch that had to be scratched, right between her shoulder blades. She felt a surge of disgust followed by a chill that moved down her back to her legs. "But if I resist this—I know I can—either way I'm dead." She felt torn by two competing urges, and she froze in her spot. "He's standing there waiting. What should I do? I'm dead, I know it. I am dead."

So Mamsi hesitantly approached the evil man and spoke. "I have heard of you so I know I shall die today. I decided it would be better to die by giving you pleasure because you are a Brahmin. Please let me go home first, and I promise to return to your house tonight."

Yavakri laughed at her pleading voice. Her misery gave him more satisfaction than he knew the sex would. "No, not tonight, woman. You may go home, but I will expect you in one or two hours. Don't keep me waiting longer." He turned and walked away merrily.

Back at her home Mamsi set about her preparations while sobbing softly. She chose a somber sari in which she expected her body to be found and slathered herself with a whole bottle of perfume. Her husband heard the noises and came into her room. When he found out why she was crying, he flew into a rage. "That's the last straw. I don't care if he is a Brahmin—he has bewitched his last victim. Now listen, dear wife. Get me some sacrificial butter." He purified the butter and performed oblations for the god of fire, Agni. Taking fine sand, butter, ground sesame seeds, barley, and sacred grass, he began to mold a figure while chanting, "O Agni, animate this form with your beloved nymph Preni. As I adorn her for Yavakri, give her life so that she may save me. Amen."

Shortly after the words were spoken, the nymph opened her eyes, then moved. She was the very image of beautiful Mamsi, except for one detail. She had hair on the soles of her feet. "Go to Yavakri,

Preni, and do what he tells you!" commanded the husband. The nymph turned and left. Mamsi's husband then took some more butter and repeated the ritual to Agni, but this time he brought to life a ferocious, jealous gandharva who was carrying an iron club. As soon as the gandharva roared to life, Mamsi's husband pointed in the direction of the departing nymph and told the creature, "Your wife just went to Yavakri. He lives over there."

Yavakri was delighted to see Mamsi arrive in her most lovely jewelry and smelling like a grove of fruit trees. He spread out the bedding, but then noticed that the woman was smiling. He scoffed, "Why are you smiling, little woman?"

"Why should I not smile?" asked the nymph.

"Because you are going to die. That's why!"

The nymph showed her teeth again. "Ah, but you have never lusted after a woman like this!" She held up a hairy foot. The Brahmin merely shrugged and took the nymph. She willingly lay beneath him, unlike any of his previous victims, he thought. But suddenly, on a hidden impulse, Yavakri turned over and saw the gandharva towering above him, blindingly bright and scorching with rage.

"Please don't kill me, sir!" cowered the Brahmin. "I know this looks awful. Please tell me how I can make this up to you!"

The fiery gandharva stared at the whimpering naked man and hissed, "You have until dawn to behead every living creature that your father owns.

That might save you." He paused, then added with a low rumble, "Then again, it might not."

Yavakri's father owned a whole village with farms full of livestock. The villagers were bewildered at the sight of the master's son rampaging through the yards, killing everything in sight. "Let's tie him up—he's gone mad," they said. But Yavakri's father stopped them. He told the excited villagers that Yavakri must have his reasons—who knows, maybe this apparent madness was divine inspiration! He was, after all, a gifted Brahmin. "Leave the boy alone!" he finally ordered.

One of the villagers, the woodcutter, was deaf, and he did not hear that order. When he saw the young man chasing and slaughtering the animals around his house, he feared for his master's property. He grabbed his ax and killed Yavakri with one accurate blow.

"So that was the end of Yavakri?" Asked my grandfather. He was still riding alongside Gotama, his servant.

"Well, some people say it ended in such a way. But others say Yavakri kept on killing animals even as the sun was rising, and then the gandharva found him and killed him. Either way, he died that day."

"Then what happened?" My grandfather asked, and Gotama finished the story.

When King Maundibha heard that his tormentor had died, he gave instructions to repair the place of sacrifice and told his priests to perform the horse sacrifice again. As the ritual began, however, Yavakri's father arrived and took the same seat his son had previously occupied. Crouching there, he loudly challenged the king. "Maundibha, I see you have not learned. You're still making mistakes in your ritual. Do you call yourself a nobleman? I know you cursed my son—but don't kid yourself. You had nothing to do with his death. Your curse is impotent—the boy simply reached the end of his allotted time."

"Your son was an evil man, sir," answered the king boldly. He was worried about offending another Brahmin, but fatigue loosened his inhibitions.

Yavakri's father seemed more gloomy than angry. He nodded—it was an undeniable fact. He conceded the fact and repeated, "I know Yavakri had his faults, but let me reassure you that you did not kill him. He was killed by his own actions."

Maundibha stared silently at the Brahmin. The old man raised his voice again. "Of course, the curse of Yavakri will come to pass, Maundibha. Because your ritual is flawed, you will soon die and your descendants will become servants. That's what I came to tell you." Then he got up wearily and left.

"So you see, my friend," Gotama turned to my grandfather, "I am the victim of that Brahmin's curse."

"But did the king die?"

"I don't know. I suppose he did, at one time or another everyone dies. Who can ever say whether life is meant to end or has been ended by a curse? A life span is far more mysterious than one's position in society, don't you agree?" The two men continued riding and discussing serious matters of fate and chance.

As soon as the old man stopped speaking, I sat down on a step. It was a flat slab, so my legs stretched out awkwardly, but I didn't mind. I was sure I had stepped on glass or that a stone had cut me to the bone. But when I checked there was no cut—just a psychedelic red-and-blue bruise the size of a silver dollar. I felt disgusted with myself, with my weakness.

The guide sat next to me, grunting as he eased himself down onto the step. "I see you're having a crisis, my friend. Don't feel bad—most pilgrims do at one point or another." He reached into his cloth bag and fumbled around until he found a flat aluminum can—it looked like an old shoe-polish can with the label removed—and opened it. "Here, I have a lotion you can rub on your feet as long as you're not bleeding." The lotion looked like tar, but had an oddly familiar smell that I couldn't identify.

"What is it?" I ran a finger through the buttery substance, rubbing it between thumb and forefinger.

"Oh, it's an old remedy, made mostly of date palm sap and some gum resin. Don't worry my friend, just rub some on your feet."

I felt silly and rude at the same time. Something about the texture of the cream made it feel defiling, even on my burning feet. Then I rubbed it on. "Is this one of those old magical remedies I'm always hearing about in Varanasi? You know, dead lizards and fish oil?"

The old man laughed at my undisguised contempt, which he must have thought a bit bombastic under the circumstances. "Do you smoke?" he asked, surprising me.

I said I did not, and he reached back into his bag. Again, he poked around for a while, then pulled out a piece of folded-up old newspaper, which he carefully unfolded. There were three hand-rolled cigarettes in there, the kind you can buy individually in kiosks everywhere in India. He put one of these in his mouth and methodically folded the others back inside the newspaper, which he returned to the bag. Suddenly he struck a match—it had been concealed in his surprisingly large hand—and lit the cigarette. He inhaled deeply, rolling his head backward and closing his eyes in pleasure. I was mesmerized by all of this; it seemed so out of character for him.

Before exhaling he looked at me and winked. Then he blew out a perfect ring, which drifted in my direction and began to expand. As it approached me, it became wavy, like a flower petal. Then, without taking another puff, he blew another ring, which moved quickly into the first ring and settled inside it. Then he blew another and another. There were now four concentric rings of smoke, and he quickly poked his finger into the rings and rotated his hand. For an instant—I couldn't even be sure I saw it—the smoke formed a perfect *yantra*, or ritual geometrical design, this one a star with flower petals around it. The next instant it disappeared.

"Did you see her?" The old man smiled proudly.

"What?"

"Did you see *her?* That was Kali. She was right there, before your very eyes. Did you miss it?" Then suddenly, "How are your feet?"

The pain was gone completely, and my feet felt almost cool. I watched the old man finish his cigarette; there were no more tricks. I wanted to ask him about the smoke pattern and what he had called it, but felt that I'd be falling into another trap. So I kept quiet and relished the painless moment. Then I started to suspect that he was waiting for me to speak, so I turned back to the story.

"I liked your story, but I have to say that the woman with hair on the bottom of her feet was a bit spooky. What does the hair mean?"

"It doesn't mean anything, my dear friend. She's a chimera with a small manufacturing flaw, that's all." The old man laughed at his own wit. "Her stuffing was showing . . ." Then he looked at me sharply and asked, "Can you tell me where your stuffing shows?"

That sounded like a *koan,* a nonsensical loaded question. I thought he was asking me about my weaknesses, maybe bad habits. Then I recalled that the nymph was made in a ritual, and I tried to calculate what the equivalent ritual that fashioned me might have been, and what the substance was. Of course, the stuff that went into making me was not grass; it was something biological and social, regulated by education and rules. Which would leave the stuffing as the vulnerable point, the key—like the solar-love flower—to unmaking my identity. If I could find that, I would then have knowledge of the mystical technique by which to create a new identity, a Kali in cigarette smoke in the world of maya. All of this came to me in a blur—it was too much to understand clearly.

"Do you mind if we resume walking? My feet feel fine now."

The old man nodded silently, maybe thinking of another way to ask his question. Instead, he simply said, "Let me tell you another story."

FRIED KINGS

King Karan was very popular among the residents of his capital city. Every morning, as the market came to life at city center, he would personally supervise a group of servants carrying a large bucketful of gold for distribution to the citizens. Each day Karan made a vow that until that bucket of gold was given away, he would not eat his breakfast. Of course, this was an astounding vow—his many doubters expected the king to go broke or break the vow in no time. But neither happened. Not only did he continue to find gold for distribution each and every morning, but he was a man who showed no anxiety, looking chubby and jolly day after day.

Months and years passed by as every morning this ritual continued: a frenzied tumult in the city market followed by a serene breakfast at the palace. What the skeptics could not even imagine was that the king's generosity depended on his ability to tolerate pain and on the great power of a cannibalistic Tantric sorcerer. Every morning, before the sun showed itself beyond the eastern mountains, King Karan would silently walk over to the house of a recluse on a hill outside of town. There, the kitchen would be ready with a large vat full of boiling cooking oil, into which the king would lower himself and fry.

As soon as the king was well done, nicely browned and crisp, the sorcerer would use a large fork to remove him and proceed to breakfast on him. He would eat the entire king, cleaning off the bones and smacking his lips in pleasure as he licked the grease off his fingers. When that was done, the great magician would assemble the bones and, using a special spell, he would restore the king—a bit stiff but otherwise fine—to life. He would pull a magical coat, which was just a dirty and patchy garment, out of the closet and then shake it vigorously until a bushel of gold coins came clanking out. These would be gathered up by the contented king and dragged back to town.

That was the deal, pure and simple. The king allowed himself to be fried and eaten, the Tantric sorcerer provided the gold, and the citizens of King Karan's city got richer. Everyone was quite happy. Of course, it was a painful ordeal for the king. At first the sizzling burn of the oil tormented him to the point of despair, and he dreaded his mornings. Eventually he became accustomed to the pain and to the repeated death. He even hummed or whistled as he walked up the hill, entered the kitchen, removed his shoes and clothing, and immersed himself in the oil vat.

However, King Karan was not the only exceptional king in that region of the country. Another was King Vikramajit, who ruled in the beautiful city of Ujjain. One day, his gardener told him that a pair of pure-white swans landed in his garden. The king hurried outside to investigate why the birds so honored him with a visit. He saw the pair looking forlorn and immediately instructed his gardener to feed the birds.

"I tried, sir," said the gardener. "I gave them grain, but they wouldn't touch it."

"This is correct, Your Lordship," said the male of the couple. "He very graciously offered us a meal of grain. But you see, we are from the great Mansarobar Lake, where all the swans have lived for generations, feeding only on fresh unpierced pearls. A drought has now dried the supply of pearls in the lake, and so my dear wife and I flew away, looking for fresh pearls elsewhere. Pearls are all we eat, Your Majesty."

The king was impressed by the dignity and beauty of the two swans and touched by their plight. He promised to feed them as best he could and immediately ordered his secretary to bring a basketful of pearls. The swans thanked him effusively and ate to their heart's content.

This continued for several happy weeks. One day, as a basket arrived and the swans calmly ate, they noticed that one of the pearls was pierced. They reasoned, correctly, that the king was running out of pearls. This made them sad, not for themselves, but for the dear king who had been so generous with them. They both knew it was time to fly away and search for food elsewhere. King Vikramajit tried to persuade them that his store of pearls was holding up, but one early morning they were gone. As they flew over the countryside, they sang Vikramajit's praises, matching the rhythm of their majestic wings with the glory of his illustrious name.

That is what King Karan heard one day, as he was getting ready to distribute the gold. "What is this?" he thought, looking up. "Who is this king? I fry myself every day and no one sings my praises, let alone the birds in the sky!" In a jealous pique he ordered his bird catcher to capture the two swans. As soon as he had the birds caged up, he demanded to know who this King Vikramajit was and what had he done to deserve such praise. When he heard what the swans had to say, he immediately summoned plates full of pearls for his forced guests, but to no avail. They would not touch the precious food.

"A righteous king, which you pretend to be," said the female swan, "does not imprison innocent animals. With King Vikramajit we were honored guests, free to come and go as we pleased."

King Karan, noble and magnanimous as any rival, or at least as circumstances allowed, released the female. The beautiful bird took to the air and immediately flew back to Vikramajit's palace. There she breathlessly told her benefactor everything. The king wasted no time and set out to rescue the male swan. He knew that if he was to avoid war, he would have to act discreetly, so he entered King Karan's capital disguised as a simple servant and obtained a position at the royal palace. Every morning he helped carry out and distribute the gold among the cheering throngs of citizens. He realized early on that such a vast quantity of gold could be obtained only through unusual means. On a hunch he began to follow King Karan, and his efforts paid off when one morning, before dawn, he spotted the king on his way to the Tantric magician.

Vikramajit stealthily approached the window and peeked in just as the king was gingerly lowering

himself into the boiling vat of oil. He saw the sorcerer testing the king with a fork, eating him
greedily, and licking the bones, and, finally, to his
amazement, he saw the assembly of the bones turn
back into the chubby old king. Then Vikramajit saw
the filthy rag of a coat yield its crop of gold coins. It
was then that he came up with his plan.

The next morning King Vikramajit woke up before
anyone else. He went to the kitchen and prepared
himself for cooking. Using a sharp knife, he slashed
his entire body till he was marked with hundreds of
bleeding cuts. Then he made a special curry mix
using salt and pepper, spices, ground pomegranate
seeds, and pea flour. He rubbed this seasoning all
over his skin, working it nicely into the cuts. Smelling
like a rare Kashmiri tandoori, he showed up at the
house of the Tantric sorcerer. The old magician was
short-sighted and failed to notice that his visitor was
a different man, but he loved the new smell. As soon
as the oil vat began to sizzle with the new dish, the
diner made impatient smacking sounds and rubbed
his hands in relish. And the taste, the taste was too
exquisite to describe—better than ever.

That morning the magician could barely keep
from eating the bones as well. He managed to stop
only by thinking about the next day's meal, but by
then he had munched down the king's right large
toe. Embarrassed by losing his self-control and feeling guilty, he said, "You were so much tastier today,
Your Majesty. What has changed? Tell me how you
did it and I shall give you whatever you want."

The king told him that since the frying was so painful, he decided that he might as well taste good. He promised to spice himself again the next day. But then he added, "I'd like to have the coat. The gold is so heavy—why not just let me have the coat? I promise to return next morning." The magician, who was getting drowsy now, gave him the coat, and King Vikramajit returned to town, limping on his right foot.

An hour later King Karan came as usual, whistling and kicking up stones. He let himself into the house, but the old man was in bed, napping contentedly under his covers. Oddly, the large vat was empty and cold, though a strange smell lingered near it. Karan called out and woke up the sleeper.

"Who are you?" asked the drowsy magician.

"What do you mean 'Who are you?'? Who can I be, you old fool? It's me, King Karan, your breakfast! What's going on this morning?"

"I already ate you—have you forgotten?" mumbled the sleepy man and turned over. "You were delicious today."

The king was stunned. "That was not me, idiot. What did you do?" he cried out loud. "Get up and eat me now!" He shook the figure under the blankets, but it was no use.

"I can't eat. I'm stuffed . . . Come back tomorrow."

"In that case give me the gold. I must have the gold." But the coat was gone and the king, devastated and feeling betrayed, had to return to the palace empty-handed. That morning he found enough gold in the treasury and ate his breakfast. But the next day he had none. The citizens were surprised—they had become accustomed to charity. Many planned their budgets expecting the daily windfall, added rooms to their homes, purchased horses on credit. Now they quickly became angry and started to chant obscenities at the king. The poor man spent the day fasting in his quarters, and by nighttime he was starving.

As another day went by in sorrow and hunger, the new servant came into the king's private rooms and tried to persuade him to eat. "Your Majesty, the kingdom depends on a healthy monarch," he said sensibly. "It is better that you break your promise than jeopardize the future of the royal house." The king said nothing, so his servant continued. "Sir, don't starve yourself. It's a slow and painful death. So many people who love you will be heartbroken, and the gods will frown on this waste of life." Although he used every means of sweet talk and common sense, Vikramajit could not persuade the visibly upset king to break his vow. He was impressed. Returning to his own room, he fetched the coat and brought it to the royal quarters. Then Vikramajit revealed himself to King Karan, showed him his foot, and told him everything. Then he said, "Here is all the gold you need, good king. You may keep the coat—but only on one condition."

King Karan did not hesitate. "Tell me what it is, and I shall immediately comply."

And so the male swan was released, and King Vikramajit left King Karan with the coat. The latter no longer resented it when the swans flew away praising their liberator. He now realized who the greater man was. Although he allowed himself to be fried for the sake of his reputation, the other was fried and lost his toe for the freedom of two birds.

I had grown up with Grimm's fairy tales, where people—usually children—were cooked and served up as food and often returned to life at the end. This story felt different because the kings volunteered to be cooked, and there was something very culinary about the whole thing—the story was almost appetizing. "I think I'm hungry!" I said.

My guide laughed. "Yes, I quite agree, and I'm a vegetarian! Would you like a little snack? I have an apple." He fished a red apple out of his bag and broke it in two, and we ate in silence for a few moments. The steps were unusually steep, and several were broken with sharp edges. The lotion was still giving off its magic, but that made my back feel worse. The scattered clouds in the west coalesced into a distant bank—then I saw an Indian robin dive over a bush, dropping a little white load.

"Do you know why fruit tastes sweet and looks appetizing when it's ripe?" I asked the librarian, now playing the role of guide myself. He shook his head. "Trees have a deal going with the birds and other animals—'You can eat my fruit, but carry my seeds in your gut till they're ready to come out!' It's quite clever actually: tree and bird together."

The old man laughed at this and said, "That's the smartest thing I ever heard about bird shit." Our eyes locked then, and we both threw away the apple core at the same time.

Then he asked me, "So what do you make of that strange little tale I told you?"

"It's clearly about self-sacrifice. Agreeing to undergo pain, even death, to achieve your goals."

"Which are?"

"Fame in the case of one, compassion in the case of the better king."

"Of course. Now, isn't it strange that the kings die—fry—and then come back? Don't you think their sacrifice would be more impressive if they just simply died?"

"That's true, but I expect there's some kind of resurrection symbolism here. If you're a good Christian, like my Catholic mother, death and rebirth are the highest currency of holiness and sacrifice."

"That's quite impressive. Your mother sounds more and more interesting all the time, if I may say so. But notice how important food is in this tale. The first king cannot eat breakfast unless the magician eats, and the second king is consumed with the need to feed the swans. And there's more. The swans eat expensive pearls, while the citizens receive gold as part of their king's generosity. So there must be some hidden connection between the kings' willingness to cook themselves and the welfare of others, which takes the form of treasures. Do you see all of that?"

"I do, but what does it mean?"

The guide looked around till he found a small bush with dried twigs. He broke one off carefully and, as I waited, he began to pick his teeth. "Sorry, young man. Apple always gets stuck in there."

Finally, he spoke. "You might wish to read it as a lesson in psychology, a story about who we are and who we want to be, or about the 'I' and the 'me.' The 'me' is ravenous and must always be fed in order to survive. The 'I' is the one who tries heroically to feed the 'me' its most precious commodity. Do you wish to guess what that might be?"

"I don't know. Self-esteem? Will?"

"Consciousness, young man, consciousness. Unfortunately, the act of feeding 'me,' who is a social creature, consumes the 'I' to the point of death. That means that the true self gives away its consciousness to the 'me'—it becomes dissolved in or identified with the invented self. It dies. But you should know that this death lasts only an instant, the 'I' must be reborn immediately in order to feed the 'me' again. So it takes on a new life in the new instant that follows its depletion, and the cycle goes on and on."

"Is the whole thing inevitable? Does it go on forever?"

"No, not once you get a hold of the coat. I believe the story hints at a solution by contrasting the two kings—their motives—and by offering true compassion as a model of going beyond this cycle. But it's just a hint—the story is no more than that."

I sat down again, vainly trying to conceal from the old man that I was tired. My feet were suddenly hot; they seemed to melt into the stones. But that was not the worst of it. It was my lungs again—the air seemed too thin and hot to provide my brain with oxygen. I felt light and transparent, dissipated into the hot sunlight and weak. I needed some shade; I yearned for water. Again, the old man showed no obvious concern, but looked through me in his unwavering, intense manner. He told me to rest and said he was going to get some water; there was a small spring down a side path. As he shuffled slowly away, I couldn't stop thinking about what he had been saying about the self and the ego, the "I" and "me."

Those weeks in the hospital in Staunton had had a devastating effect on my ego. I was twenty-six at that time, and it had taken years to cultivate a solid, if not shining, sense of self-worth. Unfortunately, half of it was tied up in what I thought I had achieved, and the other half, in what I was planning to accomplish in the wide-open future. Some of this was intellectual, but too much got invested in my body. I had been a high-level amateur soccer player, all-American in college. I had always moved easily, like an athlete. I climbed the trees for the electric company despite the fact that they paid the ground crew just as much. It seemed only natural that I should climb.

Once, in high school in Tucson, I did a research project on desert scorpions. As usual, it was a monumental job; it had to consume me—so I could win that National Merit award. I collected dozens of specimens from the Sonora Desert south of Tucson—turning over rocks and stones and gathering up the scorpions in jars for measurement. There were the pale wind scorpion, the giant desert hairy scorpion, and even the lethal *Centruroides sculpturatus*. Largest of all were the African scorpions my father—also a biologist—had smuggled in from Ghana. I kept them in my room—my folks lived in a tiny house near the campus. Every now and then some would get out and terrify my mother. I lost several to her broom. Mother never came into my room during that semester, and she kept her killer broom with her whenever she came near.

One day she had had enough, and she almost raised her voice at me—she never yelled. Her curly black hair seemed unusually wild that day; she looked younger, crazier. She accused me of trying to assassinate her. She even stooped to make the ultimatum so many sons have heard from their mothers about one thing or the other: "It's me or them, mister. Take your pick!" So I ran into the room and brought out one giant desert hairy specimen. It looked the most ferocious, although it was not. Then I stuck my hand in the jar and let it sting me—keeping my face calm just to prove to my mother that her life was not in danger.

The scorpion affair came to an abrupt end when one of the huge African scorpions got loose in the house. Mother locked me out along with my father. The two of us sat on the front steps for hours, wondering when she would back down and let us in. Eight hours later it was I who caved in, and the scorpions returned to the desert.

For weeks after my fall from the tree, I lay suspended in that contraption that kept my back in the air. Everything I needed required the help of strangers. They took turns coming in, just voices and efficient touch, not persons. I was meat on a rack. Sadly though, I felt neither humiliation nor shame, not most of the time anyway. My day was filled, almost completely, with pain, the fear of pain, or drugged semiconsciousness. It was not the sharp, throbbing, idiotic pain of the scorpion sting. This pain was my life itself—I woke up with it and spent the whole day wrestling with it. There was no place for me to hang my ego. There was no center, no room for the observing witness, which is who we usually are when we experience the world as though it were around us. At the center was just pain, and next to it, coming and going, coming and going, the fear of more pain.

There were only twenty minutes of grace each day, always at mid-afternoon. A single wintry sun ray made its way through the window, struck the rear wall, and glided slowly the full length of the room. Suddenly, as it reached a mirror, it exploded into golden fragments that showered me with imagined warmth. That show lasted only moments, followed by a gradual softening of the light, until the room sank back into darkness.

I refused to let my parents visit. The thought of my mother's demonstrative anguish frightened me, and I didn't trust father to keep her in check. It was a hard time for Mother; her letters were confused and mournful about my shutting her out.

The doctors put me on morphine and anti-inflammatory medication. That meant either sleep or drowsiness. Eventually, as the healing progressed, I was given antidepressants and willow bark extract, which is what I was taking when the hospital spit me out onto the streets of that lowly Virginia town. I had a choice to make: return to my apartment in San Diego, where I was studying, or move back into my old room in Tucson, at least until I got well. I opted for San Diego, though studying was out of the question. Instead, I floated between narcotic insensibility and chronic pain, with depression as my best friend. Mostly, though, I just waited for Rony to pull me out of that hole.

"Here's some cool water, my friend." The old man's voice jarred me, and I was suddenly embarrassed that he had gone to bring me the water. It should have been the other way around. I thanked him and drank the sweetest liquid that had ever run down my throat—cool spring water.

THE TEST

An ascetic once arrived at the doorstep of a king named Kushika. The king immediately recognized him as a holy man and showed him into the white stone palace. The ascetic strolled into the great entry hall without a glance at its grand fixtures, then announced that he would like to move in and stay with the king for an unspecified length of time. His exact words were, "O faultless man, for some time now my heart has desired to reside with you."

The king was taken aback by that unexpected declaration and confessed how childish he found it to be. "Nonetheless, holy one, I shall do as you command," he quickly added.

The sage smiled to himself. He told the king that he was tired and would like to be refreshed. The king, now joined by his wife, led the holy man to a gem-covered rosewood seat and brought a bowl of jasmine water for washing the holy man's feet. The sage allowed one royal servant to wash his feet as he cooled down beneath a fan waved by another. In the meantime, the scent of fine incense pervaded the room for his olfactory pleasure. After the guest was thus refreshed, the king brought him some honey to sweeten his palate.

Then, with visible trepidation, with hands folded, the king betook himself before the great man and said, "Tell me, O holy one, how I may be of service to you now. Whatever is mine you can have. The palace, my wealth, my very throne are yours to enjoy if you so wish."

The ascetic was clearly pleased with the king. "I do not want any of your things, noble king. Your wealth, power, and women do not interest me. What I would like is this: I intend to begin a special vow and I would like you and your wife to serve me unconditionally while I am thus engaged."

This request filled the king with joy, and he immediately agreed to serve the excellent sage. The king summoned his wife, and the royal couple led their guest to his quarters in the palace, where a comfortable bed was neatly prepared. The sun was past its midday point, and the guest announced that he was hungry.

"What kind of food would the great sage like?" asked the queen.

"Bring an appropriate snack for someone like myself," he answered vaguely. The two hosts hurriedly withdrew from the guest's room and ran to the kitchen. They returned shortly, personally bearing trays with sliced fruit, cheeses, and sweets. As the holy man indifferently picked at this and that, the couple stood tensely by, waiting for his instructions. To their relief, the guest said nothing critical.

Now he seemed to be getting drowsy. "I should like to take a nap now," he yawned. They were about to leave, but he stopped them. "No, stay here. Sit by the bed as I sleep, and whatever you do, do not leave and do not wake me up. Oh, and one more thing," he added as they sat at the foot of his bed, "I should like it very much if you massaged my feet while I sleep." Immediately, the king began to rub the holy man's feet as the latter settled into a deep slumber. It was afternoon and the sun was beginning to set. Neither king nor queen left the room, and they took turns kneading their guest's feet.

The entire night passed by in such a manner. The guest slept peacefully, while his royal hosts quietly continued to work. Another day came and then went, and the holy man slept away as the king and his wife diligently kept their promise to the ascetic. In such a way, sleeping deeply and not moving even once, the man remained motionless for twenty-one days and nights. Suddenly, on the twenty-second night, the holy man bolted upright, his eyes glazed, and without acknowledging the presence of the royal couple he left the room. Then he swiftly walked out of the palace. The king and his wife were mortified. Delirious from hunger and sleeplessness as they were, they managed to run outside after the holy man. They tried to keep up with him, but through his yogic powers he suddenly vanished.

The king fell to the ground, struck with grief and fear. The queen, however, remained calmer and helped him to his feet, and the two resumed the search. They looked everywhere around the palace walls, but to no avail; the holy man was gone. The royal couple slowly retreated back into the palace, worn out and depressed. Avoiding their servants, they dragged themselves into the guest bedroom and there, on the bed, was the saint stretched out and sound asleep. He seemed exactly as before—he showed no signs of having moved, other than the fact that he was lying on his other side. The couple resumed rubbing his feet, invigorated with relief. In such a manner, slow as the march of ants, passed another twenty-one days.

Finally the ascetic woke up. Stretching his stiff limbs, he announced that he was ready for a bath. "Rub my body with oil in preparation for the bath," he ordered the king. Fragrant oils were brought, and both king and wife began to rub the ascetic's entire body. The man sat on the bathing stool, luxuriating under the strokes of this four-hand massage. As long as he gave no sign of wanting to end the treatment, the royal couple worked diligently in silence. But once again the ascetic startled his hosts when he stood up and walked into the bathing room, where the highest-quality bathing soaps and scrubs had been prepared. Before the couple could follow him in, he vanished into thin air.

This time the king and his wife did not panic, but began preparation for their guest's meal. The most sumptuous food was cooked and delivered into the holy man's chamber. There were several dishes of venison and fowl, vegetables steamed in herbs, fried patties made of rice-banana-jaggery gruel, rice, and spicy dhal. Numerous types of sweetmeats and exotic fruits were also brought on jeweled trays. The holy guest emerged from his bath and took one look at the royal feast that lay before him. With one wave of his hand he caused it all to explode into flames. "I didn't ask for food—you need not have bothered."

The king showed no sign of anger or impatience. Instead, he lowered himself before the guest and asked how he could be of further service. The ascetic, looking at the king with intense curiosity answered, "I want you, along with your wife, to yoke yourself to one of your chariots. Then I should like the two of you to pull the chariot, in which I shall be riding, throughout the city."

Hearing this request, the king eagerly inquired, "Which chariot shall it be, sir, a pleasure chariot or a battle one?"

"Make it your heaviest chariot, the one you use to charge into enemy fortifications," the holy man answered, adding, "and make sure all your weapons are loaded onto it: the darts and javelins and golden columns and poles and standards and flags as well. I want it nice and heavy." After a pause he added, "You shall pull it wherever I guide you, slowly or quickly, and do make sure everyone in the city comes out to see you and the queen pull it. Oh, and one other thing. From the chariot I shall distribute to the crowd anything I choose out of your treasury: jewels, gems, gold and silver coins, sheep, and even your servants and the women of your palace. Is that clear?"

The king ran to make the arrangements. Within the hour he was strapped, alongside his wife, to the chariot. A whip cracked, and the two began to pull the heavy chariot through the crowded alleyways of the capital city. Their progress was slow, one tortured step after the other, the heavy load getting heavier with each pull. For fifty days and nights neither king nor wife had rested, and they were now barely able to move. And yet, not a single word of complaint came out of their mouths. They just breathed heavily in silence, with a smile on their faces. Suddenly they felt a sharp blow, then another. The holy man began to strike them with a goad that had a sharp point. He struck them on their backs, and then on their heads and cheeks. Soon they were covered in their own blood, looking like a couple of kinsuka trees in flowering season. Still, neither one of them complained or so much as sighed. The citizens of the city beheld them with great compassion and whispered, "Look at the power of penance. The mighty ascetic is so brilliant we cannot look at him directly!"

After several hours the holy man had given away the king's entire fortune and had reduced his body to a bloody pulp. The king, in turn, joyfully kept pulling the chariot. The holy man then pulled the reigns and called on the couple to stop. He descended from the back of the car and moved in front of the two. With a soft voice he spoke. "I am ready to give you a boon." He touched the two lightly, with the tip of his fingers, and instantly their fatigue and pain were gone.

"Sir, my wife and I have felt no pain serving you. It has been our honor. We have regained our youth through this ordeal. Look at my wife; she has the beauty of a goddess. Our injuries have disappeared, and our skin is radiant. We do not require anything." The king lowered his head.

"Dear king, I have never spoken idly, and I am not about to begin now. You shall receive your reward tomorrow." The holy man showed the couple a kind smile. "You may not feel the fatigue right now, but soon you will. So return to your palace and rest. Tomorrow come back to this very same place."

The royal couple returned to the palace. Although their entire wealth had been given away, the king and his mistress were now greeted by all their ministers and servants and by all the beautiful women of the court. The palace was overflowing with wealth and splendor as though their holdings had multiplied. They bathed for the first time in fifty days and ate a nourishing meal. Then, finally, the couple went to sleep.

In the meantime the holy man retired to a patch of woods by the Ganges, a place frequented by jackals and vagabonds. There he spent the night. In the morning, when the king arrived, the place was completely transformed. Where there had been only thistles and snakes, the king now saw trees blooming with pink flowers and mansions with celestial cars. There were green meadows, speckled with yellow and red mountain flowers, and crystal blue lakes. Every imaginable bird and animal was peacefully feeding in that miraculous place that looked like the divine gardens. The king saw all this with amazement, knowing that it was created through the spiritual powers of the holy man. Suddenly he came to regard his own worldly power and wealth with contempt and found himself wishing he could renounce worldly affairs in order to become a spiritual being. However, because he was a Kshatriya—a member of the warrior caste—and a king, this was not possible.

The holy man saw into the mind of the king. He spoke. "You should know, noble king, that I came here to destroy you. I came to test you, waiting for you to lose your temper or your patience. Then, and only then, I would have destroyed you. And with you the entire caste of the Kshatriyas would have vanished. You see, I was seeking to prevent a future massacre of the entire priestly caste of Brahmins by the Kshatriyas. But you have proven yourself far superior to mere warriors—you are a true vanquisher of anger. You have mastered your own nature, which is the mark of a pure Brahmin. And now," the holy man added as he swept his arm over the magnificent world around them, "now I see that you value the creative power of the spirit. In your heart you wish to become a Brahmin."

"Yes, holy man. I recognize your supremacy over worldly power or wealth."

"Well, then, I cannot make you a Brahmin—not even Shiva could do that. But your descendants will someday become Brahmins through marriage. Your race will be saved, and it will prosper under the spiritual guidance of Brahmins."

I noticed for the first time that we were seated in the shade of a tamarind tree. Because the slope was steep, the tree never reached the majestic size of its brothers below, but its canopy was broad, formed into a huge bonsai shape by the northern winds. It was a beautiful spot, but I hated the story.

"What a vicious story!"

"Don't you mean, what a vicious Brahmin?"

"Well, both. What's the story saying anyway, that we prove our worth by putting up with capricious cruelty? That we gain something by acquiescing to injustice without putting up a fight? I don't buy it." My guide seemed genuinely surprised by this display of emotion. I might have been venting, though, because the magical date-palm lotion was beginning to wear off my feet.

"You sound almost like Job railing against God, if you don't mind that I compare myself with God." That made me laugh. This tiny wrinkled man in his brown polyester pants and worn-out rubber thongs—what a startling and comic image! Then he added, "Are your feet hurting again?"

I ignored the question and attacked. "I suppose you're going to tell me that the story is merely symbolic, that it has nothing to do with Brahmin exploitation of the lower castes, right?"

This made the old man squint at me. "If you know what I'm thinking, then you tell me what I might say the story symbolizes. Go ahead. You're in a feisty mood—tell me."

I was no religion scholar—that's Rony's field—but it seemed obvious. "Mortification of the flesh. Asceticism for spiritual goals."

"My goodness, there's your Catholic mother again! We don't use this kind of language—'killing' the body. It's not the enemy you know . . . But then, you're not very far off, I must admit."

"Hey, thanks. I'm not used to agreement from you. But that doesn't change the fact that you're getting ready to maul the story in that mystical way you have of reading stories."

My sarcasm only seemed to make him happy, and he said, "Do you mean 'reading' or 'telling'? Well, why not? We 'maul,' as you put it, we interpret our life all the time. Why not do it with a story?" He saw my skepticism and took a deep breath. "Look back on your own life: your childhood, your injury, all the events that are part of your life, not someone else's. What makes it your life and not theirs? The hero, of course—the central character, the constant witness. That's you, right?"

I nodded quietly, curious to see where he was going.

"Whether you tell your life to someone else or you carefully keep it concealed—as you prefer to do—in reflecting back on it you give it the shape of a story. At the same time, any given memory that you have, any moment in your life, means something, does it not? At the very least it belongs in *your* narrative rather than in someone else's. This is your pilgrimage, not the old man's—he's just the . . . what shall we make me? The quirky guide . . . that sounds good. A bit typecast, but good. Are you still with me?"

I nodded again.

"No event in your life is a simple objective fact. It always means something to the memory-processing mind: 'This is when I started suffering,' 'This was my best day in high school.' All these judgments are literary interpretations, my friend, no more and no less. The only difference is that you are interpreting your own private symbols instead of a book or a story. But why not do the same thing with the stories I tell you? Pretend that they are part of your life. They are, after all, a part of mine."

"Yes, I see that."

"So with your permission I shall maul the story, but for your sake I'll try to be conservative. Here goes. It's a story about giving up the things that keep us back: food, sleep, sex, money, pride. Although the Brahmin is depicted as a vicious man, that's nothing compared to the difficulty of renouncing those things. So you see, it's not a story about self-torture. That would be too easy and superfluous. It's about letting go of entrenched desires. You must learn to control that constant urge for something more, something always better, more pleasurable, more important. For you it may not be money or sex, but your pride, my son, your pride. With your permission, I would like to rest a bit longer."

We sat quietly for a few moments as I tried to calculate how he came up with my major sin and whether I should pout. But then he interrupted my reverie. "Have you ever meditated, my friend, or practiced yoga?"

His comment made me eager to speak, and I told him that after leaving the hospital I took a yoga course in La Jolla, California, twice a week for over a year. The physical therapist had said it would do my back a lot of good. The students were mostly admiralty and faculty wives, tanned women with tightly pulled back blonde hair—it was a morning course. There were two instructors. Suzie, who was fanatic about "wellness" and a balanced life, never left me alone because she claimed I needed to learn how to release the tension in my body. The other was Ananda Devi or something like that. Her thing was *nirvana*—she kept telling us how close we were all getting to that blissful state beyond the cycle of all suffering. After class everyone would meet at a strip-mall café for coffee with milk foam, and the conversation would turn to famous gurus and life-altering diets. I always had espresso and a sweet—it gave me a kick in the pants and a taste of nirvana right there and then.

The old man laughed and congratulated me for being self-deprecating. "You're quite right to see the humor, young man. Yoga has produced its share of comedy. Here's an amusing little tale I once heard."

LOVE FOR THE DEAD

A man spent many years studying yoga with a guru. He became quite advanced in the Hatha school, mastering many difficult positions and learning to still his mind. But he refused to renounce the world in order to seek final liberation. His guru would plead with him, "As long as you merely practice yoga but remain a married and professional man, it is as though you are rehearsing for a play. You must leave the world behind if you wish to seek what is real."

"How can I leave?" the disciple would ask. "My wife and my children depend on me for support."

"They will be fine," his guru insisted. "You can make sure in advance that they will be taken care of."

"That may be true, sir, but my wife loves me so very much. I can't just abandon her in the prime of life when her needs ... I mean, she loves my body so." That was the disciple's final word on the subject. Of course, his own needs went unmentioned. And so he kept putting off his renunciation.

The guru resolved to settle the matter by teaching his disciple an extraordinary yoga trick. That evening the man was found in his room lying motionless, in an awkward position—arms and legs stuck in every direction. He was dead. The house exploded into wailing and sobbing—the wife cried out loudly for her dear husband. "Oh, sweetheart, where have you gone? Why did you leave us so suddenly?" she collapsed sobbing.

Friends and neighbors gathered; they felt an urgent need to perform the final rites for the good man, before ritual pollution pervaded the house. Avoiding unnecessary discussion, they carried him to the door, but would you believe it? His body did not fit. Due to his awkward posture, the doorway was simply too narrow. One of the more resourceful neighbors hurried home to fetch his ax, returned, and quickly began to chop away at the door frame. Now the noise roused the grieving widow, who was sprawled on the floor in the next room, and she came running in. Despite her violent sobs she managed to inquire about the racket.

"Dear madam," said the ax-wielder, "we have to cut the door frame. The corpse—I mean, your husband—will not fit otherwise."

The woman surveyed the situation through a screen of tears. She then addressed the man, who seemed ready to swing again. "Please don't cut the door right now. I am still grieving. He only just died." She let out a sob, then another. After some time she added, looking around the room, "You know, he was a dear man, but he did not leave us with much. I shall now have to work in order to support the orphans he left behind. We'll manage somehow, I know we will, but ... I will never be able to repair that door." Now she sobbed deeply. "Look, he died because it was his fate to die. There is nothing one could do. He's dead and gone. I think you had better cut off his arms and legs. That will get him out the door, don't you think?"

As soon as these words were spoken, the husband sprang awake from his deathlike trance. He stared at his wife in disbelief, then turned and went to join his guru.

"Well, my friend, how do you like this joke?"

The story was predictable, I thought, but his telling of it was a riot. He had contorted his wiry body—face included—into a ridiculous position and hopped on one leg as he told it. "It's cute, very cute. But is it even about yoga? I mean, it seems like a story about false love."

"Yes, good. But that's precisely what yoga is, no?"

That's it. He was doing it again! He was observing the pattern of my thinking just so he could use it against me. It was always a surprise—but I always resented it too. "I thought yoga was about mastering the body—where's the false love?" I struggled to keep the tone of my voice even.

"In a secondary sense, yoga is about controlling the body. But the goal of yoga is to still the mind, stop its fluctuations, its nervousness. And because the body is the mind, it is a body in the mind—do you understand?—controlling one helps the other. That's what the story is about."

"I don't understand that at all."

It felt like the old man was actually trying to confuse me. It was really a simple little moral parable. He calmly explained. "The story seems to be about discovering that your wife does not really love you and that therefore you are free to leave her and renounce. That's too sordid—don't you think?—even a bit silly. Would you prefer to think that if she did love you, then you would not be free to practice yoga? Hardly, I should say. The wisdom of the little joke here is that the man's idea of what constitutes practice, whether it is learning physical contortion or spending time with a renowned guru, this entire method can be the worst obstacle to realizing the truth. The wife's love in the story is the symbol for the thought that accompanies practice. If you meditate or practice yoga, thinking the whole time, 'If I just do this correctly and long enough—and hard enough—the reward will appear around the corner.' That thought, that mental construct—that's what the love of the wife represents here. You need to get rid of that before the most difficult technique comes to mean anything—if in fact it ever does."

That seemed reasonable enough to me. I've been to yoga classes with people who were full of great ideas, or worse, full of themselves. "Okay, I see the point. It makes sense, but I don't read the story that way at all."

As usual, the old man remained completely composed in the face of my stubbornness. "That is perfectly fine with me. Why don't we rest some more. This is a nice cool spot." We sat quietly for a few moments, and then he spoke again. "Perhaps that story was too brief and ambiguous. Let me try to clarify by telling you another story about this theme."

MY UNCLE IN HELL

A very long time ago, when my grandfather was only a boy—perhaps sixteen—the most important man in his life, his maternal uncle, died. Nupur had been one of the leading knights in the king's court in the capital of Kuru, where my family lived before they moved south. Kuru in those days was densely forested with banyan and nim trees, and it was criss-crossed by the many tributaries of the Krishna River before it begins its long meander through the coastal plain. It was a magnificent country where the sun and water conspired to satisfy every appetite—from the lowliest ants to magnificent tigers, and from daring hunters to meek old herbalists.

Nupur taught the boy how to handle and ride horses, even in the forest where they get so easily frightened by animal sounds and by ghosts. He also taught him how to shoot, first at targets, then at animals, although the boy did not share his uncle's thrill in hunting. He preferred to practice the other skills his uncle had taught him, such as identifying plants and mastering their qualities. The boy quickly learned how to distinguish renuka leaves from the leaves of winter cherry with its horse aroma. The first would kill you in half a minute while the other would help you gain weight or would take away the ache in your knees if you're old. Before long only the sprites of the woods, the *rakshashas* and the *nagas,* or the rare surviving old demoness knew the plants better than the boy. Everything he knew that was important to him came from his uncle. Nupur was closer to the boy than his own father.

The sudden death of his uncle threw the boy into deep grief. Immediately after the funeral rites were completed, securing for the deceased a safe passage to other worlds, the boy retreated to the woods. He spent weeks living on roots and berries, revisiting the places his uncle had shown him, spending hours in hazy meditation in which his few years dissolved into endless present moments. At times he wished to join his uncle, imagining what the afterlife might be like. In his despair he sought to imitate his uncle, so he took up Nupur's weapons in order to hunt in the dense forest.

One day, while halfheartedly hunting, he spotted a chital stag feeding on darbha grass at the edge of a forest clearing. The boy was downwind and had a clear shot. But as he raised the bow, a figure suddenly obscured his view of the animal. The boy lowered his weapon and squinted in disbelief—it was his uncle! He stared dumbly, shook his head, and mumbled, "Have I gone crazy?"

"No, you're not crazy. It's me, your uncle," came the words from the figure.

"But are you not dead? Does this mean that I have suddenly died?"

"No, my boy," Nupur smiled. "You have not died, and you will not die anytime soon. You see," he added after a pause, "as soon as I reached the other world, I began to look for the guard, and after pestering him to distraction I received his permission to visit you. All is well, my boy. Don't be sad, and stop thinking about death."

"Oh, Uncle, it's wonderful to see you!" The boy ran to embrace his uncle, forgetting that the man was dead.

When he closed his arms around Nupur, the figure dissipated like fog. The boy stepped back in shock and watched the vapors reconfigure into the shape of the man. It made no sense. "Uncle, I can see you and hear you—I mean, you are standing right before me, so why can't I touch you? Are you a mirage or are you there?"

"Don't be surprised that you can't touch me, son. The amazing thing is that you can actually see me. I am, after all, dead—a resident of hell. But trust me, this is not an illusion."

The boy's excitement deflated. His dear uncle was in fact gone. This was just a chimera, a wisp. He lowered himself to the ground and sobbed quietly. After some time he asked his uncle about the afterlife, about hell. His uncle faced him and spoke to him about his new world. "Hell is not one place, child. I believe there are hundreds of them, or perhaps hundreds of regions in one world. There is no way for me judge which it is. Each hell is perfectly matched to the people who occupy it. I have not been there long enough, but I heard plenty from a man called Bhrigu, who claims to be the son of the god Varuna.

"He tells me he has seen several of these hells. In one he saw a man cut another man into pieces and eat him. That was the victim's punishment for chopping trees in order to fuel the sacrificial fire without the proper attitude. Those trees then become the cannibalistic men of that hell. In another hell a man tore apart another man, who was screaming while being eaten. This hell was also a place for punishing mindless sacrificers, people who slaughtered and fed on screaming sacrificial animals without the proper reverence or knowledge."

The boy interrupted the description. "That's so strange, Uncle. Is hell just a place where sinners become food?"

"Oh no, my boy. That's only Bhrigu's experience. I heard of other hells with other tortures. In some, victims are burned by scorching sand or are torn apart by crows and owls. In some hells people are boiled in pots, or chopped up in total darkness, or slashed by sword leaves in a torturous forest."

"What are sword leaves, Uncle?" The boy asked this more out of curiosity than alarm. Although the hells sounded gruesome, they were remote, and he could never imagine himself there.

Nupur sighed. "Well, you see, people make their own hell. I don't think you come to a preexisting place. You make it. Or possibly, it exists but you animate it when you get there. People who are attached to sensual pleasures—insatiable sexual infatuation— go to the Forest of Sword Leaves. There they see their beloved, who beckons to them seductively. The condemned chase after the beautiful woman who quickly climbs a tree and calls from the top. Now they can't help but follow their passion. They spent all their life giving in to their desires, so they are now completely at the mercy of this erotic drive. They follow the beauty up the tree, and as they do, the leaves—razor sharp—cut their skin and flesh to slivers. Every cut stings like a scorpion bite, the pain in every inch of the body is beyond endurance, but up they go, driven by a mad lust. When they finally make it to the top, reaching desperately for the woman, she vanishes. Suddenly they hear her voice calling from below, where she stands smiling sweetly and tantalizing them to climb down. But when they do, those leaves cut them again, and the pain is as fresh as the very first slice. And so it goes, in an endless cycle of seduction, desire, and torture."

The boy sat quietly, fingering a blade of grass. He had never felt a longing for a woman, but the sorry absurdity of this punishment captured his imagination. He thought about those few times, earlier in his childhood, when he had tortured a fly by removing one of its wings. Then he remembered something else.

"So you need a body in hell, right? I mean, how could you feel the pain if you didn't have a body?"

"Yes, boy."

"But, Uncle, you don't have a body! I mean, you're more like smoke than anything else ... How can you be in hell?"

"That's what I came to tell you. It is possible to cross the threshold between life and death, or even between men and gods. But what serves as a body in the other world is merely smoke here in this life. Don't let that frighten you, because crossing is the key to immortality. Learn to do this, boy, and your fear of death and your longing for me will be overcome."

"How can I do this, Uncle?"

Nupur told the boy about a Brahmin who had known a secret chant and had sung it for him. Only Brahmins possessed the spiritual power to actually sound out the words, and Nupur was only a Kshatriya. The boy too was a Kshatriya, which meant that he would also have to find a Brahmin who might sing the chant for him. So Nupur taught those powerful words to the boy and sent him to locate such a Brahmin who would sing them. "If you do this properly, you'll be able to cross the boundary of death at will, my son."

The boy set out immediately in search of a Brahmin. He returned to the capital of Kuru and approached a group of men who looked like Brahmins: they seemed important, and aware of it. "Sirs, I am going to perform a special sacrifice that takes twelve days," he told them. "The mantras will be recited in reverse because I am not permitted to say them. Because you are learned—you look spiritually superior—you should be able to recognize the chant and sing it for me. Would any of you do this?"

The Brahmins stared at the young man in silence. They neither knew the chant nor cared to learn something that reeked of sorcery, or at the very least unorthodoxy. The boy took their silence as fear and moved on. He searched throughout the city, going from one Brahmin to the next, with no success. He began to despair of ever seeing his uncle again, when at dusk he came to the cremation ground on the banks of the Krishna River. It was nearly dark and the burning ground was abandoned to its shadows. Suddenly the boy spotted a wild man, covered in ashes, sporting long matted hair and a beard. He was holding a skull in one hand while mumbling spells as a dog licked something out of the other.

The boy cautiously introduced himself. He learned that the ascetic was a Brahmin named Pratida Bhalla. The Brahmin was a follower of a secret path to salvation, a dangerous and defiling discipline that other Brahmins deplored. Not only did he know the chant; he was actually eager to say it. As soon as the boy told him what he needed, Bhalla shrieked joyfully like a mad hyena, then promised to sing the chant during the twelve-day ritual.

The other Brahmins were jealous; they resented the fact that they were not permitted to observe the preparations for the ritual. Showing their petty side, they warned the boy to stay away from the filthy Brahmin. "He's a mischief maker," they said in a chorus, "a sinner. Be careful, boy, or he will take you straight to hell." But the boy would not be deterred, and the ritual went off as planned. The words came alive in the raspy singing of the wild Brahmin, and their subtle power began to work immediately. As the ritual progressed, the boy came to learn that mastery over death—even the conquest of immortality—required that he team up with a man who lived on the boundary of civilization and sanity. Perhaps he himself might have to abandon the values he had always been taught to respect. But seeing his beloved uncle made it worth the risk.

Just as he finished telling this story, I heard thumping sounds behind us. I turned, facing uphill, and listened. The sound grew louder, like two drums on parade. Then, suddenly, two teenage boys came flying down the steps, arms flailing wildly, tongues stuck out as their eyes were focused on the steps with a strange magnetic horror—in an instant they were below us and out of view. When only a faint tapping remained of their violent display, I whistled and exclaimed, "That was insane!"

The old man laughed loudly, then reassured me that anyone could do it. To emphasize the point he quickly changed the subject. "How did you like the story?"

"It was a wonderful story. I really like the mood: dark, a bit surrealistic, and sad. But what does it have in common with the previous story? I mean, why did you connect these stories?"

The old man was poking at the ground with his walking staff, bending down every now and then, but he heard me. "Well, the two stories share nothing at all of course, other than what one is able to discern. Here, try one of these."

From his bag he handed me a broken carob fruit that was much darker than the ones I had previously seen. I wiped it on my shirt, took a bite, and said, "You need to help me with the story. I don't get it."

The old man toyed with his own carob, but he did not eat. "In the previous story, if you grant me the arbitrary meaning I gave it, the love of the wife represented the thinking of the practitioner: 'This practice is wonderful. If I do it just right, I can expect great rewards.' In the second story we see a contrast between a very rigid notion of the afterlife—hell—and a rather vague view of immortality. By immortality I mean the capacity to move across boundaries of existence and nonexistence, the type of ephemeral power achieved by the uncle. It's an extremely old story, my friend, and this is an obscure way of speaking about the liberation of the self."

The carob was sweet and fleshy, with large pits that were easy to find and spit out. I felt elated. "That's very confusing."

"Yes, of course. Look, in my tradition the Brahmin usually represents the highest spiritual values—it's the Brahmin who possesses the knowledge that leads to salvation."

"Yes, I know that."

"But in this story the 'proper' Brahmins were useless. They were ignorant of the special chant, perhaps even afraid to approach the topic. The only man who had both knowledge and courage was regarded as polluted. He was dangerous. Do you know what kind of a man this is?"

"A sorcerer, I suppose."

"Close. He's a Tantric ritualist, or perhaps an Aghori—a mystic who follows in the footsteps of Shiva by living in the cremation grounds, where he immerses himself in secret practices that the orthodox Brahmins find dangerous."

"Would it be fair to call him antinomian?"

The old man now bit gingerly into his carob with his eyes closed, but he answered the question. "If you mean like those Christians who break religious laws to achieve mystical goals, then yes—and no. The concept you mentioned is too dualistic: good versus bad, sacred versus profane. Think of this man or woman as someone who transgresses against all dualism, against thought itself, which is dualistic by definition—'binary' is the word philosophers use. What makes our chap seem dangerous is that in straddling boundaries he questions the way we have sorted out the world: 'This is mine, that is yours'; 'I want this, I hate that.' There is nothing unlawful about what he does, and in India he has never been pursued by religious courts. We don't have your penchant for inquisitions, you know."

"So all of this connects to the previous story because giving up the thought of a goal is part of it?"

"Yes, excellent. But there is more. You go beyond giving up the thought that accompanies practice, but you also go against the very fiber of religion. It is one step further along the path—if you'll pardon the metaphor. Give up thinking about practice; go against entrenched values or desires. At the very head of the list, the most prestigious value, of course, is *moksha*—spiritual liberation. How I hate that word. You, young man, if you're a pilgrim on the path to Shiva, then you are also a seeker of moksha, are you not? Well, give that up. Abandon all thought of moksha."

I didn't really know whether I was a pilgrim or not. On that day I had no intention of performing a pilgrimage to Shiva; I was merely exercising and drying my shoes. But I was then living in Varanasi—the city of Shiva—and I cared about his river, the Ganges. I didn't know what constituted devotion or a search for knowledge—I still don't—but I was no mere tourist either. I felt pretentious but not hypocritical for speaking about such things as moksha.

But that made no sense. "That's absurd! How can I give up thinking about moksha if I'm after it? I mean, it's very clever as a paradox and all that, but it makes no sense in practice..."

"You have it in reverse, my friend. It makes no sense in theory, but works in practice. Come on, let's walk some more and see what we can make of the next story."

⟨ THE KING WHO BECAME A WOMAN ⟩

Deep in the forest at the northern end of our state once lived a king named Bhangaswana. Endowed with all the good qualities of a true monarch, he was handsome and wise, a follower of the law who ruled over a peaceful and prosperous country. Despite all his virtues, however, King Bhangaswana was unable to produce sons. He wed no less than seventeen women and was fortunate enough to father a few girls—but no sons.

In his despair he decided to perform the Agnishtuta ritual. The ritual itself was not particularly dangerous, but because all the offerings in the fire went to Agni—the god of fire—a deadly threat lurked around the place of offerings. Because the ritual made no provision for Indra, the notoriously jealous king of gods could retaliate, his quick rage ignited by the slight. And, indeed, Indra hovered above the ritual, watching the proceedings like a hawk, waiting to angrily pounce on the king for any lapse in detail. As a result of the Agnishtuta, he obtained his wishes and in a very short time he sired one hundred healthy sons. King Bhangaswana raised them happily, secure in the knowledge that his royal line would survive and the kingdom would continue to prosper.

Several years passed and Indra, who never forgets a slight, finally saw his chance for revenge. One day as the king set out alone to hunt in the dense Labha Forest, both he and his horse became disoriented and lost their way in the woods. As the hours went by, hunger and thirst further confused the two, and they wandered even deeper into the forest. Finally, they stumbled onto a clearing with a sparkling and transparent lake surrounded by ripe fruit trees and tall kusha grass. Crows nervously flew up from the branches and bees abandoned the rotting fruit on the ground when the king approached. The water looked refreshing, and the king quickly dismounted and led his horse to the water's edge. After he watered the animal and tied it to a tree, the king disrobed and entered the lake in order to perform his ablutions.

Bhangaswana dunked completely three times, pulled his hair to the back, and repeated several mantras. Then he walked out of the water to fetch his clothes, which he had left near the horse. He felt strange, and the horse twitched nervously, edging to the side as he approached. The king looked down and discovered that he had grown breasts while he was in the lake. He froze in disbelief, then turned quickly back to the water's edge. In the calm water of the forest lake, Bhangaswana saw the reflection of a woman staring back up—it was his own image! He had turned into a woman, and the lake somehow caused it ... The king felt no consolation that the woman staring back with wide-open eyes was lovely.

Bhangaswana quickly recovered from his initial shock, but was suddenly overcome with a deep shame. "A woman! A weak, temperamental, vacillating creature—just look at me!" he thought. "What will my boys think?" He reflected on his athletic boys, whom he had raised to be disciplined and upright. Then he thought about their mothers—his wives—and grimaced. "So quarrelsome and judgmental. They will never respect me in this shape. What should I do?"

Shaking and weak, the king struggled to mount his nervous horse and found his way back to the palace. People stared rudely, as they would never dare if he were still his male form. Everyone could see it was clearly the king, but it was also a woman riding that famous horse. The bustling palace came to a complete standstill, as everyone froze in midtask. The one hundred boys came running out and gaped at their ... father. The wives, attendants, and palace servants, even the dogs and the royal parrots, stood and stared at the transformed monarch.

The king dismounted clumsily, with some unwanted help, and called a hasty meeting of his family and closest advisors. He told them everything that happened, blaming fate for this catastrophe. He knew nothing, of course, about Indra's great vindictiveness. Then, crying, he added, "During my ride back I have been thinking. I can't stay here in the palace or the city. How can I possibly govern as a woman? A king must be decisive and righteous—how can I possibly live up to such lofty standards as a woman? No, I shall retire to the forest and become a renouncer, and I shall let you enjoy your lives here . . . Please try and remember me as a man." Several of the wives sobbed quietly, but no one said a word, and the king quickly left the room and disappeared into the woods.

For days she wandered in the forest, surviving on berries, mangoes, and tubers and sleeping under the dense canopy of the forest. One day she walked into the hermitage of an ascetic, a kindly man of moderate austerities. His hair and beard were long, but he lacked the fiery intensity of those god-maddened ascetics, and he invited her to stay with him. They lived together, at first as friends, but eventually as husband and wife. In the course of time she gave birth to one hundred sons, all of them as handsome and energetic as their brothers in the city.

The mother watched her boys grow, and tried to teach them as best she could about the world of Kshatriyas. It soon became clear that she was making slow progress with them, so she decided to have them educated in the palace. Bhangaswana, now called Aditya, took them to her former home and commanded her former sons to accept the new boys as brothers. The princes in the palace embraced the forest boys as siblings, joyfully sharing the life of royalty with them.

Indra saw all of this. He was still hovering over the

king he had vowed to destroy, and he now flew into a rage. "It turns out I only did this man ... this woman ... a favor. She's too happy ... That won't do." So the king of the gods assumed the form of a Brahmin and went to visit the palace. Greeted with the proper honor, he received an audience with the two hundred boys. Seeing them intermingle peacefully the Brahmin wasted no time. "How can you live together like this? Don't you realize how perilous this situation is? You don't share the same father, which means that sooner or later half of you will demand superior rights. There's no doubt about it."

The boys looked at each other. Surely that couldn't be right—they loved their life together. Still, this was a Brahmin, a respected elder. And the man continued, "Look, the sons of Kashyapa, the Creator, once fought to the death over their inheritance—the three worlds. Do you really think you are superior to them, better than the gods?" The boys now looked around uneasily, and the Brahmin kept up the pressure. He planted thoughts of jealousy, betrayal, and righteous indignation in their minds, and sure enough, eventually a fight broke out among them. The fight then grew into a battle, and within hours of Indra's arrival at the palace all two hundred boys were dead.

Aditya heard the news in her forest retreat while preparing a meal for some travelers. She collapsed on the hard ground, where she remained inconsolable. Days later the poor woman was still rolling in the dirt, lamenting her fate, when a Brahmin walked into the forest retreat and calmly approached her. It was the disguised Indra, who came to survey his handi-work. Coldly, he inquired of the pathetic woman what had happened to cause her such manifest sorrow.

The woman looked up at the Brahmin and answered, "I had two hundred sons, sir, and all were killed. They were slain by the cruel hand of Time."

"My goodness, dear woman, how did you come to have so many sons?"

So the sobbing woman told the Brahmin the story of her life. She told him about her life as a son-less king, about the ritual to Agni, her changed iden-tity in the forest. She told him about sending her forest boys to the palace and the news of their destruction. "My life is over, sir, finished—worth-less!"

Indra looked down at the wretch, who was cov-ered in dust that formed into mud stains on her cheeks. Suddenly he revealed himself to her, in his full majesty, swollen with self-righteous rage. "You brought this on yourself, Bhangaswana! It was not fate that destroyed your sons, but your own sin. During that ritual to Agni you completely forgot me, king of the gods—Lord of All Beings! Did you think I could be slighted in this manner and remain quiet? It was I who got you lost in the woods, who changed you into a woman in the lake. And it was I who instigated the fight among your sons and killed them all. And now," the god's voice reached and passed its highest pitch at once and now came down, "I am satisfied."

The woman clutched the feet of the god and

begged Indra's forgiveness. "Punish me, Lord, if you must. It was my fault. Tear me limb from limb—even death is too good for me—but please bring those boys back! They're innocent . . ." The king of the gods, having satisfied his rage, was moved by the mother's anguish and by her genuine remorse. His anger evaporated.

"Fine. I shall return half of those boys to life. But you must tell me which of them I should revive—those born to you as king or as ascetic woman."

The woman did not hesitate. "Bring back those I have borne as a woman."

Her answer surprised Indra, who could not restrain his curiosity. "Why do you make such a strange choice? Why choose the children born to you from your changed self? Please explain this mystery."

The woman did not think it was an extraordinary choice at all. "As a woman," she said, "I love more deeply. I carried those children in my body, I bore them, and I love them as only a mother can."

Indra was impressed and moved by this unexpected insight. As a reward he promised to restore all the boys back to life and added, "And you may now choose to return to your former self as king or remain a woman. What is your preference?"

"I choose to remain a woman," she answered immediately.

"But why?" the stunned god shot back. "You can have all your sons back. Then you can return to the throne, to your manhood! What are you saying? Is it the life of the forest that draws you?"

Aditya smiled and answered, "No, Your Lordship. I chose to revive my children because a mother loves best. I now choose to remain a woman because a woman enjoys the sexual act more deeply. I hope I do not offend you, sir, and all the males in your court, but having been both, I know what feels best."

Indra quietly studied the woman for a while. A number of times he opened his mouth to speak, but changed his mind. Deciding that some things are beyond even his ability to fathom, he bade her farewell and returned to heaven.

We stopped climbing next to a large boulder that was jutting out of the hill on the other side of a dry creek. A tiny stone shrine stood along the path, but I could not make out the god because an old man wrapped in rags lay curled up in front. Was he asleep? It was a fairly common spectacle, a man who may have been ill or drunk, but then again could have been in the midst of complete god-intoxication. Was there a way to tell? I returned to the story.

"That's a totally implausible story for a culture like India. I mean what Indian man would ever express a desire to be a woman? Men here have all the power, without a doubt. No, it's sheer male fantasy, something about how great it must be to enjoy the pleasure that only a man can give . . ."

The guide waved his cane enthusiastically. "Yes, a fantasy . . . It's wonderful that the story appeals to you, my friend. Can you now connect it to the previous story? What we were discussing then?"

"You mean giving up the thought of moksha?"

"Yes, that's precisely what I mean." He tapped the ground—the rags in front of the shrine stirred a bit.

"Well, there's a gender reversal here. The king becomes a woman and prefers the children born to him . . . to her, as a woman. And he also chooses to be a woman . . ."

"In a patriarchal society, correct?"

"Exactly. And switching gender or social identity is like giving up binary thinking altogether, including the thought, 'I do not have moksha, but I would like to have it.'"

"That's exactly right!" The old man's voice rose. "And what does it look like in practice?"

"What do you mean?"

"Remember, we agreed that it makes no sense in theory, but it works in practice."

"Yes, I remember, but I wasn't sure what you meant. Doesn't meditation help you get rid of binary thinking?"

"It does, but we want to go further. We now want to actually change our identity." He moved softly toward the figure in rags and bent down over it. But he kept talking. "If you are a man, become a woman. If you are rich, act like a poor man. Practice reversal in gender and in all things, and you shall move beyond binary distinctions."

"But how do I do that? It sounds far-fetched."

Satisfied with what he saw, the guide straightened up. He spoke with a softer voice now. "Yes, there are extreme forms of this practice, but there are lesser ones too. Some of our Tantric masters teach students to reverse their sexual identity during the sexual act. That is very difficult, and certainly not for you. But imagine that you are in Calcutta in April and you get on a bus that has no air conditioning. It is so hot and humid that you feel as though you are suffocating. What is the first thing you do when you sit down?"

"I open the window."

"And loosen your shirt button."

"That too."

"Next time you find yourself in this situation, do the opposite. Button up. Close the window. Feel how cold it is in there. And try the flip side too. You step out of your house in America in midwinter and it's freezing—open up your coat a bit."

"That's crazy! I don't see what any of this can do for you."

The old man ignored my protest and continued. "You are in a traffic jam and you feel angry and impatient, and then someone is trying to cut into your lane from the side—you know this situation? You move forward and block his way, correct? Why not let him in? In fact, as you let him in, give him your best smile. The angrier and more rushed you feel, the nicer you might consider acting." He smiled at me triumphantly, expecting some type of reaction.

It was all absurd—he was asking me to be a saint. "I'll just become a passive-aggressive neurotic, then explode like a post-office clerk."

The old man laughed at this—he had no idea what I really meant—and said, "Perhaps. I'm not telling you to go to extremes; just play with the situation as far as you can. Try doing the opposite of what your natural impulses tell you, reverse your habits of body and mind—eat a sweet when it's time to meditate and meditate when it's time to balance your checkbook—get into practice of exposing your rigid approach to life and see how dualistic it is. Do it in minor ways, but do it consistently, and you will start seeing through your mind's entrenched mode of enslaving you. Don't worry about a goal. Forget about spiritual goals—those are also habits of the mind."

I remained quiet.

Suddenly the guide said, "See that little cave?" He was pointing at the boulder. "Let's take that little path and see what's in the back!" He started moving toward the rock.

"But wait!" I called out. "Is that what this sex-change story is about? Reversing habits?"

"Oh, who cares? Just do the little things. Come on. This is fun!"

"But if that's all I do, how will the big things happen? I don't understand the connection between the little techniques and the big results, which I have to avoid contemplating."

The old man turned and nodded sympathetically. Then he reassured me that the big results were not so big, and that I did not have to think about them just then. Instead, he said, "Please come back here and tell me about your life after the injury—I hope you don't mind my asking. When did you first come to India?"

The path led behind the rock, around the shoulder of the hill, to a small clearing where I was suddenly treated to a broad view of the countryside west of Mysore. The clouds were amassing higher on the horizon, playing with the light of the sun, which was past its zenith. We found a comfortable spot, and I felt just fine. "By the time I got out of the hospital I was addicted to several painkillers. I was always drowsy, my short-term memory was gone, and, worst of all, I was depressed. I mean, rock-bottom depressed, almost suicidal. The yoga may have helped a bit—but not with the pain. Chronic pain is like nothing else; even when you're not hurting you're a victim. You feel stuck in your own cave, and time stops—not that it matters; there's nothing to look forward to anyway. Your best bet is sleep—unconsciousness, really—and you fantasize about death a lot.

"Anyway, Rony finally managed to get back from Pune, although the first thing he said to me was that either I went back with him or he was gone. 'I'm not your nurse—let your mom play that role.' He also said I could try Ayurvedic medicine. It might not work, but at least it wouldn't turn me into a narco-zombie either. So I went with him. Not out of optimism, mind you—there was just no other way. I was sick of my mother's long-distance nursing, the constant fussing, her own depressions. Rony felt like the sun in midwinter."

"So you went to Pune with your friend?"

"Yes. The Ayurvedic medicine was worthless, of course, but Pune got me through six months, for which I am still grateful. My friend was renting a flat in the Deccan Gymkhana neighborhood. He spent his days in the Oriental Institute, and I just wandered around and explored. In the evenings Rony would show me around on his Enfield Bullet. It was a shiny white motorcycle that ran 'taga-taga-taga,' and Rony was a spectacle riding it. He's a large, muscular man who favors white pajama bottoms and light blue kurta tops, and he wears biblical-style sandals, which he had made himself a couple of summers earlier when he apprenticed to a cobbler. He drives too fast and would look almost glamorous in a Bollywood sort of way, but on his head he wears a helmet that's no larger than a bishop's skullcap with a pink strap that fastens under his chin. I would just hang on in the back and watch him split the traffic.

"At first the sheer novelty of it overwhelmed me: the smells, the colors, the sounds. And the food—burning hot thali platters for thirty rupees, masala dosa—I loved the food. And the sunrise on the eastern Deccan hills, the film music from the small restaurant in the back of Rony's place, the cows in the street—it was such a sensory overload I was euphoric for a whole month. For days I would forget my back. But then after about six weeks the thrill gradually began to wear off, the afternoons started to drag. I got sick of drinking tea with Marie biscuits on the roof.

"Anyway, one day I had this unbelievable craving for steak: raw, juicy, rare rib eye, American style, you know. I dragged Rony out of the institute at midday and told him I had to have a good steak. Being a vegetarian, he was clueless about finding one. So we roared around town on the Enfield for an hour and ended up at the fanciest hotel in town, the three-star Blue Diamond. We ate in a polished dining room with a glass wall overlooking the hotel swimming pool. You could see the usual assortment of lobster-skinned Australians, Americans, and Germans. The Aussies were real loud. One of the women jumped into the pool in her underwear, which gave the attendant fits. He ran around the pool, balancing a huge stack of white towels in one hand while desperately gesturing at her to get out with the other. Everyone howled and guffawed at the man's puritanical upheaval. But what really caught my attention were three foreigners, studiously serene in all this madness, wearing orange robes like those of renouncers I had seen near temples. The women had short hair, and the man's hair was shaved, but there was nothing self-denying about the way they carried themselves or the self-righteous way they smiled at each other over the towel boy's petty consternation.

"'Who are these three? I mean, what are they?' I asked my friend. He had also been looking at them, and he could tell by my voice what I thought of them. Rony often told me that I was not as charitable with people as I could be, but now he laughed. He said there was a large ashram, more like a holy Club Med, right around the corner from the hotel. 'The love guru's ashram,' that's what Rony called it. Europeans and Americans come there—depositing huge amounts of cash—for spiritual training and free sex. Seriously, though, he added that they had everything there: meditation, gestalt therapy, group therapy, yoga, massage, a sensory deprivation tank, and of course the occasional glimpse of a holy man.

"'You should go,' he said during dessert. 'There's lots to do, and you look like you could use the sex . . .'"

The old man laughed. "I like your friend, he seems so much more . . . relaxed than you."

"I don't find that funny."

"Did you ever go to the ashram?"

"Yes, I went several times. But I never joined any of the groups, except for yoga for a few weeks. And, I know what you're thinking . . . I never removed my clothes. I still don't. Rony is the only person outside the hospital who has ever seen the scar."

"So you practiced some yoga. That's excellent."

"Well, there was one other thing. One day I wandered into the room where they kept the sensory deprivation tank. There was no one in the tank or in the room, only a sign-up sheet on the door with a few names. There was also a sign to hang on the door, 'Trip in Session.' So I wrote down my name, feeling very adventurous, but safe from the company of others."

"Tell me what happened."

"After showering, I climbed into the tank. It was as wide as a queen-sized bed, and I closed the two doors over my head. The saltwater at the bottom, about a foot deep, was body temperature. At first I was worried about the scar—I had heard about swimmers with cuts in the Dead Sea, which is about as salty. But the scar was fine. I lay back and felt myself floating easily. I pushed myself gently from the wall and dissolved into empty black space. I heard absolutely nothing, and saw even less. I couldn't even tell whether my eyes were open or shut. For about two minutes it was perfectly still and calm, as I adjusted to this empty environment.

"Suddenly I saw my mother's face. I mean, I really saw it—she was really there! It filled the black space, clearer than I had ever seen it. Her permanent, forced smile, her glistening eyes always on the verge of panic. The lines around her eyes deepened before my gaze, the wrinkles became grooves, and she distorted her face and bared her teeth. Then I realized she was holding her broom, and on the tip was a bright red scorpion. Both of them were staring at me, solemnly, intensely. Then her head and the scorpion in front of it started moving in my direction . . . I sat up with a start and gasped for air. There was a tightness in my chest—my mother's face was gone, but I felt suffocation. I opened the top and stood up, looking at the clock. Four minutes. I had been in there for all of four minutes! A small eternity inside was four minutes outside, in the real world . . .

"I sat back down and closed the door, determined to do a full hour, even if it turned my hair white. Even if I became psychotic—my biggest fear of all. It was a nightmarish hour, let me tell you. Every thought exploded into life with exaggerated lines. I lost any sense of what was real and what was in my mind, what *was* my mind. I saw things I wanted and things I feared, competing images clashing and gnawing at each other like mythical monsters. Whenever something scared me, fear itself had a face, and when something aroused me, passion had a different face. I can't tell you how cluttered that damn little tank was for one hour; I had not one instant of peace and quiet. The only good thing I can say about that hour is that I felt absolutely no pain. The sheer energy and terror blocked the feeble messages my back may have been sending to my brain."

The guide was fascinated by this narrative and took in every gesture in my animated telling. He nodded knowingly and said, "Close the doors to the world and the demons come right out, don't they?" He made a spooked face and wriggled his fingers.

"You could say so, I guess. But of course it's all neurocybernetics, you know, input-output."

"Ah, now there's a nice word, 'neurocybernetics.' I wonder what face that word might have in the tank? . . . Shall we go?"

FATHER SACRIFICES SON

A very long time ago—I think the British were still new here—there was a king who lived not far from our district. He had one hundred wives and not one single son. The king, whose name was Harishchandra, wanted a boy, of course, as all men do. But he was also anxious to have a son for loftier reasons. His advisor, Narada, had told him that he could expect to attain immortality or heaven only through a son. Not only would the boy bring great joy and pleasure in this life, but he would also be the ferry that would transport the king from this life to the next. But then, after he had said this, Narada added strangely, "Have a son and you shall be reborn! A husband enters his wife, and there he becomes a germ. After a full term, he is born to that mother."

The king was saddened by these words and asked the sage, "How am I to have a son? I have already tried with one hundred wives!"

Narada suggested that the king appeal to Varuna, his god. And so Harishchandra directly approached the god and begged for a son. In his despair he promised Varuna that, should a boy be born to him, he would sacrifice that very son to the god. To this, of course, Varuna readily agreed.

When the time came, a boy was born to the king and received the name Rohita. On that happy day for the king, Varuna came visiting and demanded his sacrificial offering. But the king delayed. "A victim cannot be offered until he has turned ten days old," he argued persuasively.

"Fine then. I shall wait," said Varuna, who was not a greedy god.

After ten days Varuna returned for the boy, but then the king requested that the sacrifice be postponed until the child's first teeth appeared. When that happened he asked for a deferment until the teeth started falling out, then until the permanent teeth grew back in. The boy was growing older, and the king kept putting the god off. "It is not fit to sacrifice him until he is trained in arms like the warrior he is."

When that time finally arrived years later, Harishchandra could not postpone the sacrifice any longer. It was time to fulfill his obligation. He summoned Rohita and told him about the promise he had made to Varuna. The young man would have none of it. Immediately he packed up his things and left for the woods. He stayed in the forest for one year, during which his father was struck by Varuna—who had reached his limit—with dropsy. As soon as he heard this, Rohita prepared to return, but just then the king of the gods, Indra, turned up, disguised as a traveling mendicant, and spoke. "Stay in the forest, young man. It's the best life for a future king. Trust me." The prince stayed away another year and then, as he started heading back, he heard again from Indra. The divine scoundrel again praised wandering as the supreme way of living and convinced Rohita to keep away from his filial obligations. This went on for six years.

One day, while traveling along a marshy riverbank, Rohita met up with a wild and hungry renouncer called Ajigarta. When he discovered that Ajigarta had three sons, Rohita offered him one hundred cows in exchange for one of the boys. Rohita honestly stated that this son would be sacrificed to Varuna in his own place, but promised that the father would get rich. The wild renouncer agreed on the spot, then immediately ruled out the oldest of the three. He went to ask his wife, and she excluded the youngest. That left the middle one, Shunahshepa, as the victim.

Rohita led his substitute victim—an agreeable-looking boy—back into the city and told his father about the deal. Harishchandra, who was bloated and miserable with dropsy, invoked Varuna to ask if a substitute would be acceptable. Because Shunahshepa was a Brahmin, he was actually more than adequate to replace Rohita, the god reassured him. And he added, "You may anoint him immediately as my victim."

The sacrifice was a major affair. Several famous Brahmins officiated in the key priestly roles and many distinguished spectators arrived, including the renowned royal sage Vishvamitra. But even with all these officials, no one was willing to tie the victim down. The sponsor of the sacrifice, the king, looked around, and there was Ajigarta, the victim's own father. Their eyes locked, and the ragged Brahmin spoke, "I'll tie him if you give me another hundred head of cattle." As the agreement was quickly drawn up, the man made himself busy with the ropes. The ritual proceeded. The bound victim was brought to the sacrificial pit and appropriate verses were chanted while fire was circled around him. The distinguished participants watched closely, but no one agreed to take a knife to the boy. Again the king looked around, and again Ajigarta obliged. "Give me one hundred more—that's all I ask—and I shall kill him." Some more financial details were sorted out while Ajigarta got the knife ready.

In the meantime Shunahshepa was thinking to himself, "They're going to slaughter me like an animal. My only hope is the gods. I shall appeal directly to the oldest among them." He began to silently recite esoteric verses to Prajapati, the Creator, who directed him to Agni, the god of fire, who passed him on to the solar god, Savitri; from there he went to Varuna and back to Agni, before he was finally directed to the king of the gods, Indra. The boy had addressed and praised each of those gods with great precision. The mighty Indra, who was impressed with the boy's erudition and delighted with the verses he himself had received from the boy, directed the young reciter to the divine twins, the Ashvins, who in turn directed him to Ushas, the dawn. Finally, as he was praising Ushas, each metrical triplet snapped a rope loose, and the belly of the king, still bloated with dropsy, went down. When the boy finished the recitation, the last rope came off and King Harishchandra was fully healed.

In such a way the boy completed the sacrifice that had started with himself as sacrifice, having substituted sacred words for his own blood. Then, as everyone watched in awe, the boy calmly walked over and sat down next to the great Vishvamitra, who had observed in admiration everything that took place. The boy's father, Ajigarta, came rushing over and claimed his suddenly distinguished son, but Vishvamitra refused to let the boy go with his father. "The gods," he said, "have given the boy to me."

The wild Brahmin pleaded with his son, but

Shunahshepa said, "You stood there with a knife in your hand ready to slaughter me. Everyone saw you, Father. For three hundred cows you were prepared to kill your own son, something no untouchable, let alone a Brahmin, would ever do."

"I am so sorry, my son," said the Brahmin. "Here are the cows. You may have them. I know I've done wrong."

But the boy was unmoved. "I don't trust your remorse. Anyone who can do once what you just did would probably repeat it."

Vishvamitra interrupted this exchange. "I would like to adopt you as my own son, my dear," he declared, shocking the boy who just escaped slaughter.

"How can you, sir?" the boy asked. "We don't belong to the same caste." The great man repeated his offer and promised to treat Shunahshepa as the oldest among his own one hundred and one boys and to put him first in line for inheritance.

When the fifty oldest sons of Vishvamitra, who were older than Shunahshepa, objected to the new arrangement, their father ruthlessly banished them to the most remote regions of the land. The younger fifty-one gladly accepted their new sibling as eldest and heir to their father's wealth. They were blessed with great riches and numerous children and lived in the most desirable locations of our sacred land.

We were back on the path now, having gone around a huge *Euphobia corimb* cactus with no fruit. The plant made me think of home—I needed water. I'd forgotten how hot the stone slabs were, and I just wanted to confess to the guide and climb back down the mountain. The steps were strangely polished at this point, five of them anyway.

"These five steps," he was following my eyes, "represent the five Pandava brothers in the great epic the *Mahabharata* . . ."

I could tell he was leading up to a long explanation and interrupted him, "What do you mean 'represent'? How can a step 'represent' anything?"

He looked at me in surprise—I think he suddenly saw my distress, because he took my arm and led me to the shade of a small nim tree. "Things that matter enough to us give us strength, young man, by taking our mind off of the discomforts of the road. For many pilgrims it is the Pandava steps. For you it can be the story I just told you. Would you like to sit down and discuss it?"

It worked. Something about his voice, or his touch. Maybe just sitting down in the shade. Immediately I felt stronger, more focused. "This is the second story you've now told me about murderous fathers—it's a big deal for Indians, it seems! I guess you really are like us after all."

"You must be referring to that wonderful biblical episode of Abraham and Isaac. You're quite right, we do like to tell these stories."

"You're probably going to tell me the story is not about fathers and sons at all . . ."

"What, then, am I going to tell you it's about, my friend?"

I felt his energy level rise, as though he was waiting for the setup to the punch line of a good joke. "You're laying an ambush again, and I won't fall for it. If this is not about the screwed-up father-son relationship, I can't imagine what else it might be . . . I see absolutely no way to interpret it mystically, as you like to do."

"My goodness, young man, you seem to be tied up in such knots. But don't worry. Like Shunahshepa you will soon undo your ropes." The old man beamed with this cleverness, which made my frustration worse.

"Am I just dense? I mean you have given me the key so many times . . ."

"No, no, you are not dense at all—it's the key that keeps changing, and I beg your forgiveness for that. In this instance we have a story about cooking. Do you like to cook?"

"Cooking? Are you serious?" That was the one subject I did not expect. "With all due respect, what are you talking about?"

"I shall take that as a no. Frankly, I'm not a big cook either. I have a weakness for roadside samosas, I'm afraid. If you cooked, though, you would know what I'm talking about." He found his own thoughts hilarious again and giggled in delight.

"Well, I'm lost."

"All right, let's say you want to eat one of those wonderful idlis you've undoubtedly breakfasted on—we make the best ones in Karnataka. Have you?"

"Yes, they're okay."

"Well then, you start with the rice grits and the urad dhal, which you grind together, no?"

"I wouldn't know, but if you say . . ."

"Then you allow them to ferment overnight. Otherwise," he chuckled, "they taste like McDonald idlis . . . Trust me, you have to wait till the next day to boil the patties."

"I still don't see the connection to our story. In fact, I'm more confused now than I was before!"

"Don't you see, my friend? The killing of the son is the grinding of the rice and dhal, while the chanting of the mantras by the boy is the fermenting overnight. That is what our story is about."

We sat in silence for a while as I tried to absorb what seemed so obvious to the old man. I watched his sharp features profiled against the hillside. Where did he get all that assurance? And how did he come to exert so much influence on me? A retired librarian! I gave up and told him I was still lost.

Of course, he knew I would be. "The story is telling us that there are two ways to bring something about: either crush the cause to produce the effect, which will then be new, or change the cause internally in such a way that the effect is another form of the cause."

"You mean, mechanical production versus organic growth?"

"That's brilliant, my friend! My goodness, you do catch on!" He tapped his cane on the step and jerked his knees up and down. "But in the story, and in your pilgrimage here, the desired effect is not breakfast or even lunch. It is something mysterious and tricky. As I said before—it does not really exist as a goal."

"Yes, I follow that. And if the goal does not exist 'out there,' how can it come about? How can something come out of nothing? That's what the story is about."

"Good. Do go on."

"So, mechanical causality is rejected, both in the story— since the killing does not take place—and in real life, because you have shown me that what does not exist cannot come to exist." The old man nodded approvingly. "And if the cause-effect chain is eliminated in the case of moksha—or anything else for that matter—then the model has to be Sunahshepa's knowledge and chanting of mantras. It's a new vision of causality." I was very pleased with myself, but had to add, "But what that means I have no idea."

The old man was happy with my insight and sighed, "Ah, mantras, those wondrous birds of mysterious power. If you have the mantra, you need nothing else. If you say the mantra, think the mantra, or just blow it out as air—who needs moksha then? The story tells us that what has been will always continue to be, and what is will never cease to exist. The cause does not die in order to give birth to the effect. Both coexist like the breath of the word and its meaning—air, sound, semantics, power—can you ever truly separate them in a mantra?"

"So the fermentation metaphor is like mantras because the change is intrinsic and natural, and the cause cannot be separated from the effect?"

"Something like that."

"But what about the murderous father? And the adoptive father?"

"You're very persistent my friend, and there is so little time. Just remember this. It's the biological father who kills or expels his children, and it's the adoptive father who succeeds as a parent. It takes a well-trained cook to turn food into delicacies."

"And no one is born a cook?" I added, but the old man fell silent, and I knew he had said all he was going to say on the topic. I did not feel grateful for this enigmatic wisdom at the time, but I was glad that my physical crisis passed.

We were able to resume the climb, but my pace was slow—slower than that of a sixty-seven-year-old. Up ahead a young man was reaching into a tree as his girlfriend—or wife—supported his lower back. It was a large peepal tree with widespread branches running parallel to the hillside. Dozens of little plastic bags, each with two stones, were tied to the branches. High above was a huge beehive, the largest I had ever seen.

"What's all this?" I asked. "What are they doing with the little bags?"

The old man shrugged. "Love magic, I suppose. The two stones are two hearts, don't you think?" That made sense, up to a point.

"Why here? There are peepals everywhere. Is it the beehive?"

He shook his head, then shrugged again. "I doubt it. Look, this is not my field. For all I know it's because of the way the two trees are intertwined." He pointed out a khejri tree growing next to the peepal. This was the first time in our climb that I had seen the old man indifferent to something—even scornful. It may have been the magical superstition or the silly search for securing love, I couldn't say.

Suddenly he said, "Let me tell you a story about love. It's not all you think it is."

THE PURIFYING RIVER

My father once told me about a man he knew who lived in the town of Dandanagar located on the short northward turn of the Shivanadi River. This man, Vasu, had moved into the southern town from the foothills of the Himalayas—a long way to the north. Vasu was a Brahmin who had been raised in a strict Brahminical home as the older of two boys. His life had been well planned by tradition and parental expectation, but he ruined his parents' dreams when he fell in love and then married a very beautiful woman of a lower caste. Naturally, Vasu had to abandon his role in the family business and leave home with his new wife, Kumati. The couple ended up in Dandanagar.

Life was not easy for the young couple. They had moved into town with few belongings, and Vasu was unable to practice his traditional trade. Instead, he doubled as petty bookkeeper and porter for a small trade firm that moved grain, oils, and other farm products between producers and vendors. Money was always tight, and Vasu lived with constant pain in his joints. However, their frugality and Kumati's efficient management of the household allowed them to live well above mere subsistence. They even managed to put a little money aside. Still, they could not shake the constant anxiety that shadowed their every move. They both feared that their love mar-riage, in the face of tradition, was somehow immoral and dangerous. Their continued love and physical attraction for each other only made the forebodings of doom more threatening.

But nothing happened. Kumati gave birth in quick succession to five healthy boys who grew up to be energetic and smart. Vasu compensated for his own youthful indiscretion by raising his boys in a very rigorous Brahminical environment. He took them to services three times a day and insisted that they awake before sunrise in order to bathe in the river. "The river will purify your soul," he assured them. Above all, both parents repeatedly warned their children about the importance of proper marriage.

Vasu would lecture his children using shopworn aphorisms. "The best kind of marriage must be planned by the parents in consultation with astrologers and a good pundit. Never let your senses wander, and keep your emotions under control at all times. Remember, a beautiful woman can ruin your life." The wife would then chime in. "But if you must fall in love, learn to love your assigned wife." Vasu would seal the lesson with more wisdom. "It is far better that you should not marry at all then marry against our instructions. In fact, in all things obedience to parents takes precedence!"

The boys listened attentively. Their sweet character prevented them from ever questioning their parents or bringing up the obvious discrepancy between their elders' own words and actions. Over the years, as the boys finished their schooling and took on different jobs, the parents forgot their fears and began to dream of early retirement, supported by their industrious sons. To make that reality come true they began to plan for the marriages of the five young men, but all five refused to discuss marriage. Whenever the subject came up, they either protested or turned mum. Still, because the parents knew it was their duty to marry off their sons, the topic was seldom dropped for long, and eventually it became a source of tension in the household.

Then, one day, all five men disappeared. The youngest, Pancala, who was his mother's favorite, left a note telling his mother that they decided to make their own way in the world. He reassured her that he would not marry without her knowledge, but insisted on remaining free and begged her forgiveness.

"This is our punishment—it's finally come!" both parents cried. Their fears had materialized; they were now abandoned to a lonely old age. Sometime later a baby girl was born to them. She was unusually beautiful, and her parents called her Tilottama, but she was little consolation to the aging couple. Her parents raised her quickly, merely going through the motions and waiting for the day they could finally marry her off.

Tilottama grew up with no real childhood and too little love. From her parents she learned that the heart would always be trumped by fate and that her only shield against misfortune was total obedience to the law. She became a moody girl, but her great beauty drew many offers of marriage. Vasu and Kumati finally found a wealthy old Brahmin who purchased the young bride, thereby guaranteeing her parents' coveted retirement.

Tilottama had to endure less than one full year of marriage before she became a widow. Her husband left her with substantial wealth, and in gratitude the young widow took his bones to Mathura to submerge them in the holy river Ardhachandra, gaining for her benefactor a place in heaven. The river in which her husband crossed over to the next world became Tilottama's new home. She set up a comfortable household in a stone house under a gular tree near the bathing steps. There she spent long days reflecting on the morally stringent, loveless childhood that brought her to that place. She bathed often in the spiritually consoling water of the river, but it was a solemn and austere routine that brought little joy.

One day, having already changed into a fresh sari after a bath, Tilottama heard giggles and laughter downstream. Behind a cluster of tall reeds she noticed several young courtesans who were splashing in the water. There were seven or eight of them, dressed in colorful, soaking-wet saris and painted with red and golden oils that streaked down their faces. Three older women, the attendants, were standing on the shore, shooing away the boys and curious young men. Tilottama was struck by the sensuous abandon of the women in the river. She envied the grace and power of their movement as they pivoted and splashed, shaking their wet hair like cats.

One of the women waved playfully, her eyes sparkling like two drops of the river itself, and Tilottama smiled back. The woman threw her head back gaily, gesturing perhaps or just shaking water out of her loose hair. Then she returned to her friends. The young women were a troupe of performers from the royal temple—dancers and musicians in the service of Krishna. They also acted as courtesans for the king and for aristocratic guests. When Tilottama found out that they visited the river regularly, she began to join them, at first hesitantly, but in time she increased her own abandon to the pleasures of the river.

The young women embraced Tilottama quickly as one of their own. They were very outspoken about her beauty, the purity of her complexion, and the richness of her black hair. They teasingly compared her thighs to the stems of the plaintain and praised her navel, which twisted in a clockwise fashion above her small belly with its three folds. The courtesans invited Tilottama to join them in the royal temple, desiring to show her the fine jewels and clothes that the generous king bestowed on them. As a wealthy woman, Tilottama was able to resist their invitations for months. However, the evenings in her home by the dark river were lonely, so Tilottama finally agreed to visit the courtesans and watch them perform. The hall did not look like the simple Shiva temple in which she used to make offerings as a child. It looked like a palace.

The music that her friends performed in the evening was romantic and sensuous. Tilottama was thrilled by the dancing of the two women who moved like Myanmar cats around the floor, casting sideways glances at reclining men with glistening eyes. She felt a surge of excitement as she watched her friends raise their chins and turn away from the men, who gently stroked their mustaches. She went home early that night, assaulted by the clashing flow of emotions in her body. But before long she too became a dancer, and eventually a woman who mastered the arts of pleasing men.

A few years passed pleasurably as Tilottama forgot her austere lifestyle and her late husband. One day a handsome merchant named Pancala came into town accompanied by a large entourage of assistants, driving herds of livestock and bearing vast amounts of goods. He set up camp not far from the marketplace where he intended to trade. But first, as was his custom in every town he visited, he went to Mathura's many temples paying homage to the gods, offering generous gifts to the priests, and contributing to the charities of the temples. On his rounds of the temples he entered the royal Trigarteshvara Temple, where he saw Tilottama among the other courtesans.

Handsome and athletic, Pancala was already thirty years old, but still a bachelor. He was a man who invested all his time and energy in work; his short hours of leisure were spent in temples, listening to moral readings and participating in services that extol the life of virtue. But mostly women made him nervous. He was shy around them and felt too foolish to open his mouth.

Seeing Tilottama now, Pancala was dismayed to feel his heart racing and his face flush. In his thirty years he had never been in love, and the instant he had locked eyes with this beautiful stranger—a prostitute!—he lost all self-control. The very next day he began to visit the young courtesan's matron—he was too shy to seek Tilottama herself—and respectfully offered clothes, bangles, jewels, and perfume. Gradually, with encouragement from the women, his courage grew, and he started to visit the courtesan herself. He allowed himself to drift on a stream of passion, which seemed to sweep her along as well. The two fell deeply in love and, renouncing their inhibitions, they began to spend their nights locked in boundless pleasure. Pancala seldom returned to his camp before the sun reached mid-sky; by nightfall he was gone again. In this blissful routine six months raced by.

One evening, as Pancala went to the river to bathe, a sage observed him remove his clothes. The holy man, whose name was Sumantu, saw that the young man's skin was crawling with worms; they wriggled out of the pores in his skin and fell off—thousands of minute reddish creatures. The bather himself remained completely unaware of this, for the worms were only visible to the spiritual eye of the holy man. As soon as Pancala emerged from the holy water, the worms were entirely gone, but the next day they were back. This happened over the course of several days, until Sumantu called Pancala over in order to find out what kind of a man he was.

Pancala told the sage that he was a merchant from the Deccan. He came to Mathura to trade. Then he added, "I sleep in my camp at night and worship Shiva in the royal temple of Trigarteshvara." The holy man, whose spiritual powers enabled him to see beyond shallow appearances—past, present, and future—told Pancala about the worms.

"I'm sure your intentions have always been good, young man, but unintentionally you have committed a great sin. It is only the power of this river that keeps that sin from destroying you! Go back to your camp and reflect on what that sin might be."

That very same night Pancala rushed to his beloved. He knew so little about her! But Tilottama refused to speak about herself. For hours he badgered her, begged, and demanded to know, but in her shame the young woman remained quiet. Finally, when he threatened to drown himself in the river, she relented. She told him about her parents from the northern mountain region, about her five brothers who had left home before she was born, about her own short and lonely marriage, and finally how she became a prostitute. She sobbed in shame—she had never starved for food, merely companionship, she cried. In her self-pity she failed to notice that the young man—her brother—turned deathly pale. His eyes rolled up into the back of his head just before he fainted and collapsed.

Tilottama's sobbing and then her screams when her brother fell to the ground drew a crowd of worried attendants, who quickly revived Pancala. When asked why he had fainted, Pancala looked at his sister and whispered to her, "I am your brother." The poor woman immediately forgot her petty shame. A white pallor came over her face like a blanket of snow, but she gathered herself long enough to run out of the room.

The sin of incest, even if committed inadvertently, is frightful. It equals the great sins of killing a Brahmin or murdering a woman. Nothing short of self-immolation in the flames of a funeral pyre can remove that evil. Everyone knows this, including the brother and the sister, who avoided each other now, separately preparing for their own destruction. Tilottama gave away everything she owned: jewels, clothes, and real property. She left only enough to finance a large pyre at the riverbank. Her brother also donated his considerable wealth to charity and religious institutions. He bathed in the river in preparation for his fiery suicide, but first he prostrated himself before the feet of the holy man Sumantu and confessed his sin. "O guru with the vision of gods, you were right. I have committed incest with my sister, whom I had never known. The worms only you could see were the sign of my hidden guilt. I beg your permission to immolate myself in order to remove the stain from my family and avoid the tortures of hell."

The holy man remained quiet, while Pancala waited. The young man was desperate to know how his violent death would repair the injury of a sin. What was the mechanism—the correlation between sin, pain, and redemption? However, his questions remained unspoken, and he assumed that the holy man had nothing to say to a defiled sinner. Brother and sister then walked firmly toward the burning pyres, determined to do the right thing, which neither understood. Just then a booming voice was heard from the crystal-clear sky. "Stop!"

Pancala looked around—there was no one there. Then he saw that Sumantu, still sitting at his spot upstream, was motioning for the two of them to approach. They turned away from the flames and joined the sage, who finally spoke. "The voice you heard was the god of this great river. Obey it! Do not immolate yourselves! Although fire and its pain have always purified sinners, your sin has already been washed off in the holy waters of this river when you bathed for this ritual. That which the fire achieves through pain, this river accomplishes through compassion."

Pancala looked at Sumantu in confusion; he had never heard of such a thing. But the old man nodded in reassurance. "You have to accept this fact, even if it contradicts what you know. But now you must remain by the river as a renouncer, without wealth or worldly attachments. Bathe daily and study with me, and you will go to final salvation. Your sister will discipline herself by this river in the same manner, and she too will someday move beyond the world of death and rebirth."

Down below us now, the young woman giggled and shrieked as her mate stumbled back. Both were flailing their arms wildly, as though waving something off. But they were laughing, as people often do when they are embarrassed by their fear of bees.

"You know, I'm amazed at how pervasive this fear of incest seems to be, as though all of us are susceptible to it at any moment. Our Oedipus slept with his mother. Your Tilottama slept with her brother. It's always inadvertent, but so inevitable. At least in your case the consequences were not so tragic."

"Quite right, my friend. We don't have your stomach for the tragic, the irremediable."

"Actually, I find that to be a disadvantage from a dramatic point of view."

"Of course, I understand. Still, you might feel differently if you allowed the story to speak to you directly, at the place where you are right now."

"What do you mean?"

"Well, you're moving up the mountain, over halfway up to Shiva's temple. You have overcome some hardship and heard a few things about practice and about the goal—it's time now to start reflecting about that."

"I'm trying. Mostly I don't know where you're leading me."

"The story I just told you is about false discipline in meditation. You see this in the depiction of the parents."

"You mean, because they are so preoccupied with training their children to do the very opposite of how they led their own lives?"

"Precisely. That is willfulness in the application of discipline. With regard to the body, this means starving it or hurting it. Even putting on the distinct garb of a 'holy man' or a swami perhaps—like those three tall figures by the pool in Pune—can be such false discipline. In meditation practice this means applying willfulness to control every aspect of the body's actions: a ramrod back, regulating the inflow and outflow of breath through the proper nostril, tweaking your fingers just so."

"But isn't that precisely what India is known for? I mean meditative technique—yoga, *sadhana, vipassana* . . ."

"Yes, no doubt it is. Hence the boy—who symbolizes this in the story—has accumulated bountiful wealth."

"And what about the girl?"

The old man winked at me. "Ah, the sibling of the body: the so-called mind. She is the young widow who has replaced chastity with prostitution." He removed his woolen cap and ran his fingers through the white hair. There was no sign of sweat. "Years ago I knew a man who entered a distant monastery, thousands of kilometers from his hometown here in the South. He spent five years in constant meditation facing a wall, and then he came back. When I asked him about his progress in meditation, he told me he had made none. 'For five years I sat quietly,' he said to me, 'trying to discipline myself. To be honest, Bhaiji'—that's what he called me—'every single minute I spent thinking about sex. The harder I tried to control the body and purify my thoughts, the more rebellious did both become. My improved concentration only made the erotic images more vivid. I could see women in every detail, feel the pleasure of copulation, suffer the regrets of abstinence. There was no point keeping up the charade, so I left.'"

"So the girl represents preoccupation with sex or desire?"

Slowly, with measured precision, the old man put his cap back on. "Not at all. Sex is just a symptom for something else, and the girl is the mind that thinks itself separate from the body, able to control the body. The result is profound agitation. It does not have to be centered on sex; for other people it is money, fame, health, regrets. When you meditate, the mind—clothed as the ego perhaps—wants to act like a bossy landlord: 'I am in charge here. I control the breath. Every thought is mine. I need to get all of this chaos under control.' It's just you sitting there, but that little voice acts like a feudal king. As that mind accumulates mental powers—improved concentration, for example," the old man laughed as though recalling his own experience, "it gets harder, not easier. You must learn to let go of the idea that the mind is separate from the body."

"Okay, I see that. But what is the incest at the heart of the story?"

"The incest represents the greatest danger of all: the pretense of a false unity between the mind and the body."

"Wait, let me get this straight. Before, you said that the boy and the girl are the symbols of body and mind as separate entities, and now you are saying that the incest is the symbol of a false unity?"

"That is correct."

"So, which is it? Are the mind and body separate, in which case they can be united, or are they the same, in which case their unity has to be false?"

"That's wonderful attentiveness on your part. I commend you. But why speculate? As long as you *think* that your mind is separate from your body—whether it actually is or not—the unity you try to establish in practice will be a false one—it will only produce worms."

"And if I think that the mind is united with the body?"

"Also worms."

"What are the worms, then?"

The guide faced me squarely and spoke very slowly. "Worms, my friend, are the types of mental agitation—fantasies, fears, rage—that are experienced as though in the body. In India some people call them ghosts; to you they may be psychosomatic experiences or even delusions. Even the Buddha had an intense encounter with them in his meditation."

"Well then, if the worms are delusions and impurities, what is the river that purifies them?"

The old man looked at me silently. With one hand he pointed toward the top of the hill; with the other, holding his cane, he pointed to the bottom. Then he resumed walking.

Off to the west a crested hawk eagle dove silently, just as another bird screamed. Suddenly it changed its mind and bounced back up, using an updraft only it could know about. A field mouse was hiding somewhere with its little heart pounding furiously. Behind the averted drama the clouds were moving closer to the mountain, though twenty degrees of open sky still separated them from the hot sun. The old man was also studying the sky, raising his head after each step, before he began his next story.

SHIVA'S FOOL

My granduncle first met Sangayya one day as he was riding with the king's entourage to survey the space between the banks of the Godavari River and the mustard fields. "Something useful ought to be done with all that land," the king would repeat like a mantra. Granduncle—Tataji—was finance minister and general advisor to the king, the only man in the court who could be counted on to speak his mind.

The boy was thirteen or fourteen when Tataji saw

him that early afternoon crouching under a huge almond tree, staring up and scratching his head. An instant earlier a pair of jungle crows, responding to the nervous energy of approaching horses, flew out of the tree, tearing a green almond off its stem and dropping it next to the boy. In his days and weeks under that tree Sangayya had never seen a green almond actually fall off. The dried almonds, pecked and eviscerated by birds, seemed to belong to the soil under the tree, while the perfect fuzzy ones remained contentedly on the branches. Frozen in his attentive crouch, waiting for a sign perhaps, the boy attracted my granduncle's attention, because the old man had observed the small chain of events and was fascinated by the boy's singular attention.

Tataji was a great soul, a heroic devotee of Shiva, a man who saw god in all things. In the thin, undersized boy, whom everyone regarded as a moron, he immediately recognized a pure simplicity, a delicacy of consciousness that not even the tiny sparrow possessed. That night he made some inquiries and discovered that Sangayya's parents simply let him wander about, thinking him too simple for either schooling or work.

The boy spent his days roaming or just daydreaming near the river. For hours he would sit by the banks of the Godavari, lowering himself under bilva or banana trees into the tall weeds. He had a favorite anthill into which he would gently poke a small twig, allowing a few ants to explore its length and watching one or two daring ones venture onto to the hand holding it. To Sangayya they were not fire ants or red ants, but only "ants," the anthill was the ants' "home," and the almond twig was just a stick. He saw the ants in great detail, each with its own personality, appearance, and walk. He addressed them individually—but it is hard to say what they replied. No one knew what the world looked like behind those wide black eyes and perpetual smile. He spoke simply, using the most general nouns, but spent hours studying the minutest details of life around him. He lived in a buzzing world of small organisms and fragrant plants in a richness where not a speck of perceptual space remained for emptiness and abstraction. His mind could have been the laboratory for ancient Vaisheshika philosophers who speculated on what is more solid—the particular object or its class. But for the boy, that wide space between a thing and its name was a mysterious and vast universe, later to be filled with the presence of Shiva.

Despite his busy schedule, Tataji began to spend afternoon hours with the boy, watching the breeze ruffle the leaves—my granduncle explained that it was the wind that made the blades of grass bend in the same direction at the same time. Sometimes they dozed, or Tataji would tell Sangayya stories about his own childhood, about gods, or about demons and sprites. The boy loved the stories of Krishna's boyhood and Rama's heroic adventures. But surprisingly, his favorite stories were about Shiva, and over the years he developed a curious love for the tale of Shiva in the pine forest. My great uncle told it repeatedly, never in quite the same way and always simply.

"A very long time ago, much before our grandfathers were born, but not so long ago that the world was young, the great sages lived in the Himalayan mountains in a pine forest. They lived there with their wives, but they took vows of austerity. Some stood on their big toe, others remained immersed in freezing water, while yet others dined on moss alone. One day Shiva came to pay a visit to these great men, but they could not recognize him. This was because he was stark naked and completely covered in ashes, with his markings erased. His eyes were wild and red, he had crooked teeth, and his hair flew about as he moved. His penis and testicles were covered with red chalk. He yelled and laughed or smiled mischievously while dancing erotically, bewitching the wives of the sages who had come out to see him. Meanwhile, his own wife, Parvati, matched his every move.

"The mighty sages, who had accumulated vast spiritual powers through their hot austerities— enough to destroy a god—began to curse him, calling him an ass and a demon. They were outraged by his vulgarity, by his disrespect for their way of life— their dharma. They cursed his penis to fall off.

"The great god only smiled at their rage and responded, 'No one has the power to remove my *linga*, but if your wish is to castrate me, so be it.' He disappeared before their very eyes, having first removed his own linga.

"The world, bereft now of God, quickly sank into chaos. The sun went cold and the seasons lost their rhythm. The sages tried to return to their blend of asceticism and domestic routines, but they became uncertain about how to balance their duties, so they lost their virility. In their confusion and despair they sought out the divine grandfather, Brahma. They told him about the naked madman with the crooked teeth and vulgar dance moves, about their curse, and everything else that took place before their world fell apart.

"That ancient god marveled how miserably such distinguished men had failed to recognize the supreme Lord, the creator, sustainer, and destroyer of all the worlds, master of the great eons. Was it any wonder their world had come undone? Brahma instructed them to create images of the divine linga, perform rituals of propitiation for the god, control their anger at all times, and learn to master the inner self. The sages returned to the pine forest and worshiped the linga image of Shiva for a full year.

"When spring came around again, Shiva returned to his original form and visited the hermitage, which was now lush with trees and vines, awash with the colors of hundreds of flowers, and alive with buzzing bees. The sages were quick to recognize him this time; they praised him calmly, with hands pressed together above their heads. With the lightest smile, the great god accepted their pleas for forgiveness offered along with garlands of flowers and perfumed incense. Shiva assured them that those who delight in the ashes of the Lord shall have their sins burned away, having obtained the highest fulfillment from God. He taught the sages how to perform the Shiva worship with the icon of the linga using perfumed water, blades of holy grass and flowers, and many other implements. Since then the sages have been able to follow their austere vows and maintain the life of householders as well. They became established in their dharma, knowing that God was pleased with them."

The first few times Sangayya heard this famous story, he said nothing but stared intently at Tataji. He asked to hear the story again, insisting that Tataji repeat every detail. Gradually, as the years passed and the boy heard the story hundreds of times, he would start to giggle and ask questions. "What is a linga? Do I have one? How could the linga just fall off? Why were the sages so angry at the naked man? Why was it so hard to be an ascetic and a married man? Why did the world become chaotic when God disappeared?"

Tataji patiently answered all the questions, over and over again. He began to take the boy, then the young man, to the large Shiva temple in town, where he showed him that the bewildering linga worship was merely a simple devotional service to God as honored guest—a bathing followed by feeding and refreshments. "Sometimes God is our guest," he would say, "and sometimes we are his." He took Sangayya to the bathing steps on the banks of the river in town where holy men covered in white ash, with long matted hair and bloodshot eyes, bathed near the burning grounds, just as the story had spoken of the god himself.

Over the years Sangayya became consumed with Shiva. He knew nothing of theology and hardly anything at all about dharma or the law. But he developed the habit of covering his skin with white ashes, and he chanted the many names of God whenever he remembered, repeating them with every inhalation and exhalation, replacing his previous silence with a quiet stream of divine mantras. He learned to use bel leaves as an offering to Shiva when he was in the forest, where—alert as a deer—he was always on the lookout for rudraksha trees. Sangayya was never seen without rudraksha beads, which he made himself from the fruit of the tree. His beads were polished brown, always the size of large figs, and always with the perfect five grooves between the thorns. Gradually, that vast space that separated the world of discrete objects from the world of names filled with the energy of Shiva. Sangayya's simple consciousness became increasingly God-centered until he saw Shiva in all things.

Evenings in the city descended with the smoke of cooking fires mixed with promises rising out of fragrant incense sticks. It was the wake-up time for thieves and adulterers, while for Sangayya evening marked the time for linga worship. He observed noblemen carrying flowers and fruits, along with betel leaves, valuable clothing, and ornaments—all wonderful ritual offerings to Shiva—as gifts for their mistresses. Sangayya, who knew nothing of sex and less of prostitution, congratulated them on their devotion as he watched them admiringly. They laughed and waved back.

Late one evening, almost ten years after their friendship began to blossom, Sangayya asked my granduncle if he could join these men. Tataji, who knew the full depths of Sangayya's simplicity, laughed and agreed. Making sure the young man was properly dressed in fresh cotton clothes with a silken vest, Tataji sent him, with a chaperon, to a beautiful and devout courtesan named Saumatri.

Sangayya had never seen anyone so lovely, other than Parvati herself, whose golden image faithfully flanked Shiva at the great temple in the city. Nor had he ever seen such a palace, with its quartz steps, gold-plated floor, pearl-shaped plaster designs made of musk, and strings of gems that served as lamps. Only the celestial mansions of Shiva could be so luxurious, he thought, feeling now that he had entered the divine realm of his great Lord.

Imagine his surprise when the beautiful woman began to bathe his feet—those same feet that crushed the lumps of clay at the river's edge—and, scandalously, now drank the water that ran off into the crystal basin! She was no Parvati. He felt a stern reproach rising in his chest, but it quickly dissolved, for she now took his hand and led him into her inner chamber, gesturing with a sweep of the hand in the direction of a polished wooden bed that dominated the room. It was covered with a down mattress and decorated with marigold and rose petals. On the floor were strewn oleander flowers, and in a crystal bowl were manjaris—mango flowers for gentlemen who needed extra help.

"Ah, of course," he thought, "this is Shiva's throne, right here in the center, and this lovely woman is not Parvati, but one of the god's attendants!" Sangayya smelled a subtle fragrance riding the soft breeze from the window, as if to confirm his observation. He looked around and found a simple blanket, which he carefully spread on the floor before the great bed, preparing a space for the ceremony.

"I shall follow the usual procedure," he announced simply, "and may I suggest that you follow my example?"

She lowered her eyes and smiled acquiescently. Sangayya then smeared white ash, which he had brought in a pot, over his entire body until he looked like Shiva. He worked deliberately, concentrating intensely as usual. When he finished he turned to examine the great lady. She had not followed his lead, but responded to his inquisitive look by telling him that she was emulating Parvati, who covered her own body in yellow ash. Then she showed him her glistening skin, oiled with turmeric massage oils.

"Where are your rudraksha beads?" he asked, pointing at his own thorny necklace.

"The dark ones are too sharp and salty," she apologized. She showed him her magnificent pearl necklace. "I have these white ones. They have become round and polished because I wear them all the time."

That truly impressed Sangayya. "Yes, I understand. Such devotion! Polished rudraksha beads . . . and look, you have one in your nose! That is completely new to me. And look again," his voice rose in excitement, "even in your hair. What a great devotee of Shiva you are!" He looked admiringly at her tiara. Saumatri was embarrassed by his undeserved admiration. She shrugged. "Only God understands these things. It's not even mentioned in the Vedas."

In all his years of participating in rites of worship for Shiva along with the village and city folk, Sangayya had rarely seen such modest devotion, nor had he ever seen such extraordinary symbols. He contemplated her form thoughtfully, then noticed that the lady's hair did not conform to Shiva's matted shape. "Your hair, madam, why don't you wear it matted as Shiva does?"

"Oh, but I do. I merely leave half unmatted to make it easier to place flowers for the worship ceremony." She turned sideways and showed him the beautiful red Chinese rose in her braid. "I also sprinkle it with ashes," she added pointing out the decorative tassels.

"Well then," he continued to inquire, "why don't you wear a truss?"

Saumatri showed him her full-length silk sari and exclaimed, "This is my truss, dear man. I cover my entire body to shield it from the eyes of nonworshipers."

Sangayya was overwhelmed by the lady's profound virtues and by the majesty of her unfamiliar school of theology. He fell at her feet and begged for instructions in the ways of her devout sect. And so she spoke to him at length, softly instructing him about Parvati's austerities on Mt. Kailasha, about her own vows following the great goddess, her learning in the holy texts, her rituals and devotions. The beautiful harlot, who normally spent her nights entertaining noblemen, spoke to simple Sangayya about the milk she used for bathing the linga along with the roots, fruits, leaves, and vegetables that nourished the divine couple. This man, who saw Shiva in all things and performed Shiva worship in all his actions, simple Sangayya, was impressed.

Looking around the great bed—to him, Shiva's throne—he saw neither sandal paste nor betel for the ritual. He commanded Saumatri to bring all the proper items for the worship and was thrilled by her meek obedience. As the flames for the offerings flickered off her necklace, bracelet, and shining eyes, the moon arose—white as Shiva's teeth. Sangayya was meticulous with every detail, but Saumatri wanted to make him happier.

She summoned seven performers into the moonlit room, all of them beautiful women carrying musical instruments. One brought her mridangam drum; another brought a clarion. There were also a drone, a flute, and finger cymbals. The two remaining women—voluptuous and radiant—began to dance. As Sangayya proceeded with the linga worship, serving Shiva all night long, the women performed and danced beautifully, starting with the rare Raga Ranjani, with its sinewy solo, which is then joined by the mridangam leading to a suspensefully prolonged syncopated beat. They played in the correct mood for the time of night, offering their art to God and their beauty to the young man.

Early in the new day's morning, the young man returned to the palace, glowing ecstatically like the fresh sun on the horizon. He saw my granduncle standing with some of the gentlemen who had returned from their own nocturnal affairs. Sangayya beamed at the group. "What an orgy! What debauchery! I can only regret, Uncle, that you were not there to enjoy the women. Please rest assured I was thinking of you the whole time. Tell me, sir, do these fine gentlemen—fine lovers, I'm sure—enjoy the same orgiastic pleasures in which I spent this last night?" He described in great detail the gorgeous Saumatri with her unusual symbols of devotion: the yellow ash, the white, smoothed-out rudraksha beads, her unusual truss and hairstyle. And he also recounted her profound theology and devotion to Parvati. The more he told them, the wilder was the laughter of the men in the group; they were all bending over, slapping each other on the back with shrill pleasure.

Tataji too smiled broadly, but his laughter was pure joy as he turned to the men. "Have you ever seen such simplicity and such strong devotion? Where else will you find a man who knows only Shiva as he seeks the pleasure of serving God above all pleasures?" The men all nodded in agreement and congratulated Sangayya.

"What a wonderful boy. I really liked him. But can you explain that space between a word and its meaning? Isn't it just another way of saying 'perception'? You know, seeing or touching?"

We had just passed by a stunted banyan tree with aerial roots that would never make it to the ground. Too much rock, I thought, and the erosion on the steep slope had to be fatal. How did the tree get there in the first place?

The old man spoke. "No, my friend, not exactly. When we look at an object, say that eagle we saw earlier, the bird we see can be only what our senses grasp. It is never the object itself—you follow this?—but only as it appears to us. The mind controls every perception. It is the mind that reaches and holds on to objects like that bird, very much in the same way that a man who is drunk on todi reaches out to hold on to something in the dark."

"You mean that we see with the mind's eye?"

"Yes, the mind's eye—excellent. Now, the name, 'eagle' or 'banyan tree'—or for that matter 'rudraksha' or 'pearl'—the name is neither completely arbitrary nor completely natural. Don't let our ancient philosophers fool you about this. You can call the rudraksha a pearl as much as you like—it will still fetch just a few paise in the market. And call your wife's pearl necklace 'white rudraksha' in Varanasi's Vishvanatha Temple and they will ridicule you as a lunatic.

"But that still does not explain the 'space' between the word and its meaning, does it?"

"Sorry, I'm meandering a bit. Language is special and subtle. It resonates between pure sound, 'AAAAH,'" the old man grunted loudly, "and pure meaning, 'ant.' One is a part of the universe like ocean waves, the other is an invented game. Words resonate between these two extremes—that means they move back and forth. They do this quietly and unobtrusively: maximum sound one instant, maximum meaning the next instant."

The old man paused for a while, and we stopped walking. He tapped on the ground with his walking cane and illustrated his words in the dirt. "Don't get me wrong. That motion has nothing to do with space, nor does it happen in time. It is more like something that happens inside a point, a theoretical place that must exist if there is to be a line, but a place you can never see." He drew a line between several points.

"And the line in that metaphor is the equivalent of the river that purifies?"

"You are a wonderful listener, but just a bit off, young man. The line too is a theoretical or conventional reality, whereas the river is Shiva consciousness. Let me give you another example. Can you say Kathakali? Ka-tha-ka-li."

"You mean the Kerala dance? Katakali."

"Yes, well, close enough. Notice when you say the word—say it again—notice how your breath behaves. Sometimes it blows free, and sometimes it stops. It stops on the 't-h,' does it not? Actually, somewhere between the 't' and the 'h.' How long does it stop?"

"I don't know, one tenth of a second?"

"Perhaps. Who can measure? But there is a point—an instant—where the stop gives way to the next aspiration. The point of absolute stop is an instant between the previous aspiration and the next one. When you say the word 'Kathakali,' the word flows out as though there are no stops, and yet without the stops there would be no word. This is a metaphor for the point of consciousness I am discussing. A whole world hangs on it, but it is only a point, less than an instant."

"Okay, I think I follow this."

"Sangayya was gifted at slowing things down to such an extent that these points stretched out, and they consisted of nothing other than Shiva himself. The instants of consciousness—mere points—were more real than the reality pegged onto the instants—convention—and for the boy this was Shiva."

"But why call it Shiva? Why not call it just consciousness?"

"Do you remember that story about Shiva and the holy men? Where the great god danced like a crazy madman?"

"I sure do."

"That's your answer, then. You see, Shiva is the most contradictory and confusing of gods. He is one thing and its opposite: divine and worldly, sexual and ascetic, sublime and crazy. He is the very embodiment of paradox."

"Wait, let me finish the thought. The instants of consciousness are also paradoxical because they do not really exist, and yet everything that does exist hangs on them!"

"Yes, bravo! That's very impressive. You see, there is no line without dots, no consciousness without either instants of awareness or the 'screen' on which they are manifest. But neither of these exists either."

I suddenly recalled my last night in Pune. I had been up for over two days due to an all-night wedding in a village the night before. My back was worse than usual, and I was nervous about the flight back home. I went up to the roof to meditate, facing west for once—away from the moon. I decided to focus on the pain and almost immediately entered a state of dissociation. The pain did not disappear, but it became someone else's pain—a stranger sitting slightly in front of me, below and to the left.

After some time my consciousness floated back in the direction of the meditator, whose back was turned to me, and entered his body. But my consciousness did not take over the body. Instead, it began to ride piggyback on the mindless body. I should have been a whole person then, body with mind. But the fit was a bit off so the body acted first and only then did my will intend to perform the act. The man stood up, then decided to stand, moved a hand to scratch, then willed it. I decided to urinate over the side of the roof, only to discover that it was already happening. I laughed, then intended to laugh. Each action took place before the thought it was supposed to obey.

The gap was precisely one instant—less than a second—but to me, at that time, it seemed huge. It was enough time for a loop of silliness that made me feel like a boy in Naples hanging on to the back of a trolley that was going very fast where it had already been. A decision emerged to decide to intend something in order to break the cycle. But that made things worse. It sent me spiraling downward, and I became dizzy and had to shake my head. I found myself sitting in the original meditating position on the roof, facing the west, still away from the moon.

I never gave this episode much thought—it didn't seem particularly "mystical" and it was hardly much of a psychedelic ride either. Now it made perfect sense—it was a bit of Sangayya consciousness.

I'm no philosopher and hardly a mystic. Important insights, what few I've had, have always just snuck up on me—like stupid thieves who break and enter to bring things in. This was such a moment, and the instant I became aware of knowing something new, I felt a gust of cool wind from the west. It ruffled my hair and dried my sweat.

"What are the other gods like?" I asked the guide earnestly.

The guide removed his woolen cap, but this time he dropped it into his bag. As the wind played with his thick white hair he said, "Let's look at Vishnu."

THE WEAVER WHO BECAME GOD

Under the mountain range, which you can see only if you go as far as the horizon, is a modest city called Pratapa-Vishama. The king of that city, some time ago, was a short and fat fellow—King Brihatsena. He was a pretentious man and even his name—"Mr. Large Force"—was pompous, for his army was minuscule. He kept only as many soldiers on hand as was necessary to put down a rebellion likely to erupt due to the onerous taxation he imposed on the poor citizens.

The royal palace towered ostentatiously over the city's main boulevard, where merchants and craftsman spent the better part of the day trying to sell their wares. If the city was known for one thing above all else, it was the excellence of its carpenters, masters of the trade who worked the ample supply of walnut and sandalwood from the nearby forests. Even competitors admitted that their boats could outlive the river, and that their cabinets were more valuable than the most precious contents. Down that main boulevard, two friends—a carpenter and a weaver—enjoyed strolling in the evenings, when the light softened and made even the palace glow kindly.

One day, on the eve of the annual spring festival, the two friends were strolling arm in arm, and the sun was beginning to set behind them. The weaver, whose name was Prasad, spotted the king's daughter standing on the balcony high up above the boulevard. That very instant he was smitten by the little arrows of the love god, Kama. The girl, Sulocana, was fair-skinned with long slender limbs, and her eyes glowed with a brilliant golden light. As the weaver looked up at her, she was scanning the street absentmindedly, completely oblivious to individual faces in the crowd, but Prasad felt as though their eyes met.

"Did you see that?" he asked his friend. "She noticed me. She likes me."

The carpenter looked at his friend with amuse-ment. "Yes, my friend, of course she did . . . and she blew me a kiss too." But teasing failed to derail Prasad's strange new obsession. He rambled on about the previous life he must have shared with the princess, fretting that the distance and barriers that now separated them undermined the handiwork of destiny. In the following days these fantasies mush-roomed into elaborate plots; to his bewildered friend all of this suggested a profound delusion. "She loves me, I know it . . . but she's locked up in that palace. I have to get there. We must unite!" Every evening was now spent loitering beneath the balcony, which was far too high to climb up to.

"You must help me, my friend," he begged—melodramatically lowering himself on his knees before his best friend. "If I don't get up there, she and I will both perish."

The carpenter was a sensible man and did his best to disabuse Prasad of these dangerous delusions. But he was also a perceptive young man who knew where to draw the line between friendship and mothering—in short, he decided to help his poor friend. And, in fact, he happened to rank among the elite carpenters of the city; perhaps he was the very best. One day he came up with a plan that required all of his great skill. He constructed an airplane that was shaped like a bird, the very image of Garuda, which was Vishnu's own vehicle. For wings he used the astonishingly light sal wood, which he sliced into thin boards. Then he made a discus that would have pleased the great Protector of the Law. Meanwhile Prasad managed to obtain the type of clothes that Vishnu might wear on a nocturnal visit and dyed his skin blue—he was a thorough and determined impersonator.

The aircraft was superb. It took off with a short run into the light breeze, gained height, and carried Prasad swiftly toward the clouds. The weaver fumbled with it for a while until he learned how to glide, rise with the hot streams, and surf the cooler drafts. Made fearless by love, he quickly became skilled enough to navigate the plane directly onto the royal balcony. There, Sulocana was stunned to witness the descent of Vishnu himself in his very own body. The god was smiling beatifically if a bit breathlessly, then surprised the girl by speaking her name. "My dear Sulocana," he said, "I flew down from the distant heavens because of your great beauty. I had to see for myself who this mortal was about whom all the divine damsels were gossiping in envy." The ploy worked charmingly and the girl proved a willing victim. They spent the evening making love in Sulocana's quarters, and thereafter the great bird landed on the balcony every evening.

One night a chambermaid could no longer contain herself and excitedly told the king and his wife about the nocturnal visits their daughter was enjoying with a great celebrity. The royal couple hid behind a curtain, where they witnessed, to their endless joy, the visit of Vishnu with their very own Sulocana. They softly withdrew from the room until the couple finished their play, but they did not go far. As soon as the weaver had settled into his little nap, he felt a soft tug on the foot of the bed, which made him bolt upright.

"A thousand apologies for waking you up, O Lotus-Foot Lord," the king huffed. "We could not help noticing that God himself chose us for his family. The honor is too great, O Infinite Pervader." He looked over at his wife, who motioned him vigorously with her hands to go on. The king, sweating and breathing hard, continued, "Of course our beautiful daughter was promised to another, to a mighty king no less, but

... that is ... you being God, that is no problem. No problem." He bowed and genuflected.

The weaver finally shook the cobwebs from his eyes and caught on. But what could he say? What would Vishnu say? He stared dumbly at his new father-in-law, waiting for a chance to put on his trousers and disappear.

"Very well, My Lord—son, I shall leave you to your rest. Please make yourself comfortable in my modest home." He followed his wife out, both pivoting stiffly at the doorstep and bowing one more time.

The next day King Brihatsena declared war on the three kingdoms that surrounded his little state. In his confidence he did not even bother to address his withered little kadamba tree, under which stood the neglected royal shrine, before setting out for battle. It was a wonderful opportunity to capitalize on the greatness of his new son-in-law—after all, the coffers were nearly empty. The three neighboring states were far more powerful than Brihatsena's ragtag army, but they surrendered without a fight on Vishnu's reputation alone, for the god was now a member of the household. A quick agreement was drawn up for handsome tributes, which made Brihatsena euphoric—for all of a fortnight. Soon he began to regret just how easily it all came, and thought about how much more he could have obtained with just a little bit more effort, perhaps even some bloodshed. So he doubled the tribute, then quickly tripled it.

The neighboring kings had avoided war because they feared taking on Vishnu—it meant certain destruction. Now they felt they had no choice; their very existence was sapped by the greedy tyrant. So all three rounded up their forces, and the combined army marched on Pratapa-Vishama. The king, wealthy beyond his wildest dreams, had by now lost all touch with reality, and he personally led his meager forces out of the fortified city to meet his enemies on the battlefield. He was quickly routed.

Bleeding, his clothes in shreds, the king managed to limp back into the city and quickly up to his daughter's quarters in the palace. "Darling," he whined, "where is that wonderful husband of yours? We're desperate for his help outside the city—it's a massacre out there. Please summon him, honey." The weaver was just then taking a nap in the bedroom. His young wife tiptoed in and gingerly shook him awake. As he stretched and yawned, she filled him in.

Prasad was snared in his own trap. He realized instantly that his day had come, that death was at hand. Moodily he stared at his beautiful, innocent wife. It's not her fault, he thought. In his heart he whispered good-bye. As the princess watched, the weaver packed up his Vishnu gear and heavily mounted the wooden contraption. He managed to take off from the balcony and, barely missing the town's one minaret, he flew over the city walls toward the enemy forces. "I am dead, I am dead," he repeated to himself. Then he began to yell, "Run away! Vishnu's coming!" raising his voice as best he could.

Far above in the divine mansions, the gods were watching the sad little comedy with interest. Vishnu's supporters had been critical of their friend for letting this masquerading weaver get away with his mischief for so long, debasing the great god's reputation. They now split into two camps. Some said, "Let him die, Lord. It's time for this fraud to pay his debts."

Others responded, "Don't let him die, Lord. His enemies think he is you; they believe God himself is flying overhead. If he dies, they will think they killed you!"

The first group responded, "He's a scoundrel, sir. If he wins today, his master will become greedier and there shall be no end to this charade."

The others said, "Find another time to stop the charade, sir. This is basically a decent man—don't let him die."

Vishnu listened carefully and found that both sides made sense. "Let me see for myself," he announced, and in an instant he became a murmur inside the heart of the weaver. He found himself inside a blindingly black, bottomless pit of terror, a fear as deep as he had never seen in his entire creation. The poor weaver's heart was imploding in his chest, sending urgent signals of despair to his brain. But deep inside was a minuscule grain of courage—a speck of determination. The Pervader of the Universe came in for a closer look at that tiny place. Suddenly he realized that the weaver was thinking, far beneath his own conscious awareness, "I shall die like a god, I shall die like a god. Even Vishnu will be proud."

At that very instant the god Vishnu saturated the person of the weaver and his flying machine with his own being—the weaver became Vishnu. He routed the invading armies, driving them noisily from the gates of the city. When his work was done, he flew back to the palace, into the arms of his beloved.

"First Shiva, now Vishnu—you know, I never could figure out your complicated polytheism."

"Well, my friend, that's a matter for another day; we are too far up the mountain now. But rest assured, this is a story about faith, not about God."

"Yes, I can see that."

"In the previous story one-pointed consciousness was the subject: the simplicity that serves as the gateway to higher states of being. But this was not the river yet, not a flow. There is still discipline and will, and your experiences, though transcendent, are still isolated. Do you agree?"

I was flattered by his tone, and I nodded, though I wasn't really sure.

"The move to the next stage is far more difficult, my friend. What comes after gateway consciousness is sheer terror, the terror of complete dissolution."

"Why is that?"

"The move from one-pointed consciousness to stream consciousness feels like death, death followed by rebirth. Some people experience this movement as exhilarating. To you it will be sheer terror."

"But why?"

"Because of your karma, dear boy, the stuff of your soul. It's not that you are too passionate, though you are. And it's not that you're too judgmental and harsh—especially with yourself. Mere habits can be broken. You are carrying a load of pain that is so deep that it makes up your very fiber. Your American psychologists might say that this pain is locked up in the deep subconscious—but that's not a very happy image—I never liked the basement metaphor. It's more like DNA: substance mixed with form. Even the burn in your bare feet cannot remove the more essential pain. You come to depend on living this way, leaning on your suffering, using it to sort out the world into good and bad, right and wrong. The move to stream consciousness ends this old pattern—and so it feels like dying."

"How do you know so much about me?"

"I know because you communicate it. Your nightmares for instance, those huge black snowflakes that drift down from a pale blue sky, threatening to swallow you. Night after night you wake up on the floor next to the bed, shivering in cold sweat, curled up like a fetus. They started long before your accident, when the flakes became fiery—no?"

"I don't see how you could possibly know about my dreams. That's uncanny . . ."

"This stage—if you make it this far—will be the worst crisis of your practice, my friend. Your brief moments of euphoria when consciousness settles down through meditation will be followed by something worse than even the fear of dying. In fact, I think death doesn't frighten you enough. This will be more like absolute dissolution, eternal incarceration in a pitch-dark closet, psychosis."

"Eternal?"

"Who can say how long? Certainly longer than you'd like.

But listen to the story. Somewhere at the core of that crisis a faith will sustain you. Not belief—that's too shallow. Belief is always about something: 'There is a god,' 'The sun will rise.' Faith is both more and less than that: a simple affirmation of being—optimism in the face of chaos. You have no idea it's there, and you must face the terror before that faith opens up. When it does, you will be flooded with divine consciousness, a radiant grace."

"Is that moksha?"

"Don't be silly. Of course not."

We climbed quietly for some time, one step after another, slowly. Then I gathered the courage to ask, "What will it be like after I enter that new realm of consciousness?"

"I can't say, and if I could, I wouldn't."

"Why not?"

"Because if I did, you would end up creating precisely what I suggested, which would eliminate the miracle of grace."

"Are you saying there is no one objective way of experiencing this state of consciousness?"

"It is different for everyone, and it can shift wildly. It is not even a 'state,' as you put it. The only thing that may be said is that unhindered consciousness obeys no rules. Some are immersed in deep love; others disappear to themselves without a trace. The possibilities are endless."

I lost track of where we were—possibly seven hundred steps up the mountain. A small wash ran directly under a thick banyan trunk on the left, exposing the tree's lower innards. Two roots clung to a rock and kept it suspended above the ground in a space that was neither tree nor mountain. The sky above the tree now matched the gray of its trunk, and the silver leaves rippled like water.

The old man broke the silence. "Listen to a story about mind. Mind only."

THE GIRL IN THE STONE

This is a story I know only because I eavesdropped on a retelling of it by someone I respect, who was telling it to someone else. I can't tell you with certainty that it's true, but as far as my own experience goes, it does have the ring of truth. It feels authentic to me, but you decide. At any rate this is exactly how he told it.

As I'd had enough of the madness into which my life had settled, I decided to renounce the hectic pace and find a quiet place to meditate. The only place I could go where no one would find me was a distant corner in the vast space of emptiness. There, using my imagination, I created a modest hut. Sometimes I meditated inside the hut; at other times I preferred to sit outside. Assuming a lotus posture, I quickly entered a trance state, and in a flash one hundred years went by.

I was awakened from my trance by the voice of a woman. It was a sweet voice, but I thought I heard a strain of agitation in it. She was either singing or calling me. I roused myself and began to search for the woman, who may have been in some distress. I searched for years, wandering through entire worlds

I had created in my mind. However, as I could not find her, I returned to the cabin to meditate. Soon I heard her playing a flute. Then she approached the place where I was sitting.

She was a young woman with flowing black hair and a creamy complexion. Before I could speak, she started to tell me her story. "My name, sir, is Anjali." Her black eyes shone at me. "I live at the very edge of the universe on a mountain that marks the border between the world and the nonworld. It's a huge mountain with vast numbers of rocks and boulders. I live in one of the atoms inside one of the stones in that mountain—with my husband.

"My husband has lived there for a long time—steadfast in his study of scriptures, disciplined in meditation. One day he realized that he needed a wife, so he created me in his imagination. I don't know why he made me so beautiful—I am the most beautiful woman in our universe—or why he bothered at all. He has remained chaste, and I have never known the joys of domestic life . . ."

"How is it possible to live in a rock?" I interrupted her. "How can you even move about?"

"We can, sir. It's a fact," she waved her arms in excitement, showing just how much room there was. "And not just the two of us. There are cities and villages in the stone, and mountains and lakes. It's a whole world in there, you know. But now you must help us," she said suddenly, ignoring my reactions. "We're facing a major catastrophe. Our world is about to explode into flames—a doomsday fire. We have no way of escaping. My husband failed to attain sufficiently high spiritual knowledge to free us, so we're trapped in that place. Sir, you are a great man. Would you please come and show us the way out?"

The fragrance of this young woman made me forget my meditation. Thinking about her impotent old husband, I agreed to go immediately. Of course, I had no idea what I could possibly do, but she was overcome with joy. The woman turned out to be a magician who could fly, while I drifted in her wake. In no time we reached the mountain at the end of the world. She took me to an ordinary round stone, but I could see nothing in it—no sky or earth, no lakes or planets or sun. All I could see was a tiny stone.

At first the woman was puzzled by the fact that I could not see her world, but then she remembered something important. "It's an illusionary world; it exists only in maya. That is why you are not seeing it. You are spiritually so superior that your vision passes right through that world. Perhaps," she suggested, "you should try to remember how such a world might have appeared to you in the past."

She was right—it worked. I could now see her world, as though in a dream. We entered it together, and she introduced me to her husband—an old man with fiery black eyes.

The couple did not embrace or even exchange a glance. The young woman repeated her request that I teach her husband higher spiritual knowledge so that the two of them might escape the approaching catastrophe, but her husband cut her short. Looking directly through me, he hissed, "Great sage, I am the one who created this universe. I have even created you—just as you have created me. This woman is caught in her own karma—she is the victim of her own powerful traces from the past. As a result she constructed a world of her own in which I am her husband. Do not believe it for a moment! I am not her husband, and she is not my wife. The only thing you may believe is that today is in fact doomsday and that with it comes the end of my own karma. I urge you, good sir, to leave quickly. Go back to your own universe."

As soon as the man stopped speaking, he withdrew his senses from the world around him. Immediately, the world lost its solidity and form, flames erupted everywhere, and a flood of churning waters covered the entire space. As I stood there watching in awe, the world in the stone was reduced to a perfectly still nothingness.

As I turned my head, thinking of the woman, I noticed that each of the stones around me was its own universe. There were millions of separate universes, each with its own history and geography. It was then that I realized that each universe was created by the mind of a single person.

I decided to return to my cabin back in the corner of the empty space. However, when I got there, I could not see my body anywhere, although I had left it behind in order to fly with the woman. In its place, I saw a magician occupied in deep meditation, having taken over the cabin. He must have looked for a special place to meditate, just as I had. Furthermore, he must have possessed high discernment in order to perceive the cabin, which I had constructed out of the stuff of my higher reality—mind only. He probably assumed that I would not return, so he disposed of my body, taking it for a corpse no doubt. How dare he do that? What did he do with my body? Will I ever find it again? And my cabin, he's trespassing there! In my anger I came up with an idea for evicting the intruder. I returned to the tumultuous world I had originally left behind and stopped imagining the space in which the cabin stood. As soon as I stopped imagining, the magician who was meditating in my space lost the solidity of his seat. He tumbled down to earth, landing roughly while still sitting in the lotus posture.

He seemed stunned and a bit hurt, for which I felt instantly remorseful. Helping him brush the dirt off his clothes, I introduced myself and asked that he tell me about himself. We decided to return to that empty space together, where I was able to find my body and reconstruct the cabin. I made it large enough for the two of us, and we shared that place of meditation for a long time.

"This is crazier than *Alice's Adventures in Wonderland;* she, at least, didn't make a cabin crash by stopping to imagine it . . ."

"Yes, I agree. It's all quite nonsensical. I'm afraid that's unavoidable when you stand outside someone else's mind, looking in. But once you get in, anything is possible. Can the madman be sure he is not a mystic?"

"What do you mean? Usually that question is asked in reverse, you know."

The guide ignored my comment and said softly, "Would you tell me about that night in Varanasi, about six weeks ago, when your illness was at its worst? I believe that was something of a turning point for you."

"How could you possibly know about all of that?" I asked the old man.

"I know everything about you."

I looked to see if he was serious, but it was hard to tell. I told him how absurd I found his statement to be—I wanted to know if he meant it.

"Look at my staff." The old man showed me the walking stick he had been carrying. It was too long for the small man, about six inches taller than he was. "Here," he said, "measure it against your height."

I took the cane and placed it alongside my body. It was precisely my height. "Please keep the staff and value it. It was made especially for you and you've earned it." He patted my shoulder as though knighting me.

"But how could you know my height? Or about my illness in Varanasi?" I refused to accept the fact that he could see into my thoughts or memory—I had nothing but distaste for the occult. But I did remember the night he mentioned, and the depth of my fever. So I told him what I knew.

The strange thing about all of this was, if Rony had not told me what I had done, I would never have considered that night unusual—at least not in the way the guide was implying. In the middle of that night—it was early in the

course of my illness—I suddenly woke up feeling invigorated and almost euphoric. In the dark I got dressed and
walked three blocks to a Durga shrine in order to thank the
goddess for my renewed health. Her image was reclining
within the inner sanctum, but that did not seem strange to
me at that time. I approached and hugged her feet, kissing
them with devotion, for I had nothing else to offer—no
flowers or fruit. Durga suddenly stood up and rested her
hand on my head in blessing, and I felt a deep joy warm my
entire body. A loving force surrounded me and literally carried me away. In an instant I woke up in bed—it was late
morning. Rony was looking at me from the other end of the
room, smiling and shaking his head.

"What a vision I had!" I said weakly. "You won't believe
it . . ."

He laughed at this. "That was no vision, friend, or dream.
In fact, you almost got yourself arrested last night."

"Why? Did it really happen? Did I really touch Durga?"

Rony laughed harder, then doubled over in laughter. Then
he came over and hugged me. "That was no Durga, buddy. I
can tell you that." Then he told me something bizarre; if it
were not Rony, I would never have believed it. In my delir-
ium I went to the landlord's house and virtually assaulted
Mrs. Sharma as she lay in bed next to her husband. Rony had
followed me and managed to pull me back in time—it was
my illness that prevented them from filing charges.

The fever and the detoxification accounted for that vivid
hallucination, so the doctor told me. But my visit with
Durga still remains a true memory, while Rony's account of
my adventure was just hearsay. The very next day Rony
announced that we were going south to Mysore for a dose
of reality.

The old man was laughing. "So perhaps you understand a little bit what I mean when I say that you are the product of my mind. I know it sounds like gibberish to you, but if you talk about it in the future, people will understand. Of course, in my world there's a perfectly simple explanation for all of this."

"Can you please explain what you mean? I'm not enjoying this."

"Here, let me tell you another story. It may help you," he said.

RULER OF THE WORLD

North of the renowned city of Mathura was a dense forest of nim, teak, and many other fruit-bearing trees as well. It was a lush place where a man could live with no fear of hunger or the threat of predators. Two hours' walking distance into the forest one could find the small town known as Salim, next to which was a peaceful forest retreat named after Shiva's wife—Gauri. In a modest but comfortable estate in the heart of the Gauri Retreat lived an elderly couple with their eight sons and daughters-in-law. There was nothing unusual about this extended family, which survived on small-scale farming and a bit of trading, except for one thing. The eight boys, though different in age and appearance, were psychically connected. Their mental bond was so strong that when one of them hurt, the others would cry. When another had a strange dream, all arose the next morning in a daze.

One of the boys, the youngest, one day saw the king pass by with his entourage of assistants and beautiful courtesans. He decided on the spot that he too should be a king or, better yet, ruler of the whole earth. Immediately, all eight brothers became inflamed with the same ambition. They all wanted to be ruler, each one the only lord of the entire world! Due to their modest station in life they realized that the only way to obtain such a lofty goal was through the power of spiritual austerities. All of them as one resolved to abandon their home and their wives in order to pursue a rigorous course of penances.

That very same day the young men kissed their wives and hugged their parents. They left the women and elderly couple crying at the door, waved good-bye to each other, and then turned to eight separate directions. Feeling that their shared consciousness was an obstacle to the desired goal—sole mastery of the world—the brothers resolved to achieve as much separation as they possibly could. And so they marched vigorously for seven weeks.

The youngest of the eight, whose name was Kundadanta, walked in a northwesterly direction for those forty-nine days. He finally stopped when he saw a majestic fig tree, as big as the mythical kalpa tree, set off from a cluster of ordinary looking beuls and ashoks. The trunk of the ancient ashvattha was twisted and braided like the sinewy limbs of an old yogi. Its branches spread high above, forming a shady canopy that covered a full acre. Kundadanta stared at this magnificent sight, smiling in delight. He spent the rest of the day preparing a rope out of the plentiful darbha grass that grew there. The next morning he slung the rope over an east-facing branch, tied the other end to his ankles, and hoisted himself off the ground. Hanging with his feet in the air and arms dangling below, he entered a deep meditative trance.

In the meantime, the eight wives at home sank into inconsolable grief. They removed their jewelry, shaved their hair off, and refused to eat cooked food. The goddess Parvati, who roamed that forest retreat like a kindly spirit, saw the young women acting in the manner of widows. Deeply moved by their devotion, she appeared before them. "I am very pleased with your loyalty and modesty. Tell me what you would like as a reward."

The wives answered in a single voice, "Please grant immortality for our husbands."

But Parvati shook her head. "I can't do that. It runs against the natural order of things. Ask for something else."

Again in unison, the wives responded, "If not immortality, then please grant that when our husbands die, their spirits may remain at home."

Parvati readily agreed to this and even added another boon. "Your husbands' efforts to rule the earth shall be successful."

The wives were so thrilled with their good fortune that they immediately vowed to undertake a pilgrimage. They chose Kalapagrama because it was a holy place for worshipers of Shiva, the lord and husband of Parvati. Wasting no time, they gathered a few belongings, remembering, of course, to invite their elderly parents-in-law. Although the trip took several long days of dusty walking, a happy mood prevailed, and they all found the discomforts of the road easy to bear. One morning they arrived at the Godavari River, where all the pilgrims had to board a ferry. The women took their place in the long line, supporting the old couple as they waited patiently. Directly in front of them quietly stood a short, stout man, whose long messy hair was flaming red and whose skin was filthy with white ashes. The young women had never seen anything so odd—they eyed the man with suspicion. As soon as the ferry arrived, they pressed their parents-in-law forward, nudging the stranger aside.

The man, however, was a powerful and ferociously temperamental ascetic named Durvasa. Instantly, he exploded in rage and glowered at the old couple. Then he spit out this curse: "Your sons have set out to rule the world. They have recently obtained boons from the goddess. Whatever boon they received will produce an opposite effect."

Before the women or the old couple could open their mouths to apologize, the man vanished. They searched frantically among the crowds, behind the stalls and kiosks, and pleaded with the dhobi women who were beating clothes against stones at the river's edge, but he was gone. The family members boarded the ferry and continued on their pilgrimage, anxious to win reassurance from the god that all would turn out well. The joyful mood was now replaced by a dark foreboding. How could the eight brothers possibly rule the world now? And how could their spirits remain at home even after they died? It all seemed lost. The pilgrimage ran its full course—the divine couple was duly worshiped—but tragically, both Shiva and Parvati remained silent.

Back at the huge fig tree Kundadanta was hanging by his feet. Time stood still for him as he journeyed into unknown spiritual realms. But time also flew by as the tree bore fruit twelve times in what seemed like one summer. After twelve years a brilliant being, bright as the sun, appeared to him and declared soundlessly, "You may stop your penance now, Kundadanta. Success is yours. Go now and rule the earth." At that very instant the ascetic felt a tug, then another. He blinked his eyes open.

A pleasant man with lotuslike palms, four arms, and a mace was gently tugging on his arms. "Holy man, are you well? I thought you looked like a corpse, but from close range I can see that your skin looks almost healthy. Why are you engaged in this torturous penance?"

"Leave him alone," came a voice from another man—this one was a fierce dark man with two arms and three eyes. In his hand was a trident. "Let him hang there. What is it to you?"

The two began to argue, promptly forgetting the hanging ascetic. "Help me down," Kundadanta interrupted the noisy quarrel. "Please, can you cut the rope?" The pleasant man helped him down gently and brought him some water. Then he began to massage the ascetic's feet while his companion was visibly trying to interrupt these acts of devotion by getting in the way.

"Sir," said the first, "you are clearly a great ascetic. May I serve you?"

Before Kundadanta could respond, the other jumped in, "Why do you want to serve him, you fool? Can't you see he's nothing but a corpse? Come on, let's go and let him rot."

Kundadanta saw another argument about to erupt, so he got up stiffly and began to walk away. "Thank you for cutting me down, friends. I am now going back home."

This seemed to upset the first one, who began to plead, "But sir, may I join you on your journey? It would be my great pleasure to serve you." He shook off his companion, who was just then pulling on his shirt, and joined Kundadanta. The two walked in a southeasterly direction, back home to the Gauri forest retreat. The fierce companion shook his head in anger, but followed the others.

The journey back was difficult. Kundadanta walked with great difficulty, and his two companions kept quarreling. As one served him with a cheerful demeanor, the other tried to sabotage his friend's efforts and kept hurling a steady stream of invectives at both his traveling companions. The ascetic often felt his anger starting to flare at the wild man, but it was quickly doused by the good cheer of his new friend. As they walked, Kundadanta told the two about his spiritual experiences, explaining why he took on such a harsh penance. He said that having obtained his wish, he was now going back to see his brothers and reclaim his wife.

The pleasant companion was awed by the description of the solar being and by his message. "Undoubtedly, sir, that has come true. I am sure that you are in fact the ruler of the entire world." He had no reason to think so, of course, but his support was sincere.

Meanwhile, the other man howled with hysterical laughter. "Ruler of the world. Ha! Ha! Look at him, he can barely walk!" He began to chant obscene meters about Kundadanta's "royalty" and only interrupted himself to pass wind at the king. The two companions broke again into one of their many fights, while Kundadanta tried to ignore them.

Eventually they arrived at the old forest retreat. Kundadanta was sure this was the place, but it was hard to tell. The trees had all turned into boulders, and the fruit into rocks. The lush Gauri ashram was now a desert. Kundadanta's vicious companion began to laugh. "So this is the lush ashram you told us about? And these rocks, I suppose, are your brothers?"

The kind companion hushed him forcefully. "Quiet, man! Can't you see this is a tragedy?" Then turning to Kundadanta, he added, "I'm so sorry, sir."

In the place where the family house had been only a single nim remained, intertwined with a mango tree. Under these was now sitting a wispy holy man, bowed by the desert wind, deep in meditation. The yelling woke him from his trance, and he smiled at the three traveling companions as though expecting them. "Hello, my dear Kundadanta. Come here, son." The young man approached the holy sage, touched his feet, and sat before him.

"You are wondering what happened here, why your home is gone and where your family has disappeared to. That is understandable. You must have patience, my boy. I will tell you everything." And so he did. As Kundadanta's two companions sat down not far away, the holy man talked about the sorrow of the eight wives, about Gauri's promises, and about the curse of the powerful Durvasa.

The three-eyed companion interrupted loudly, "Ah, Durvasa. There's a true holy man. A great man. He's as powerful as Shiva himself." He turned to Kundadanta, "Forget your boons, friend, you are certainly doomed. As you were whiling away the years on the tree, bigger things happened in the world. Nothing will erase the curse of Shiva's holy man!"

The other companion quickly responded, "Don't mind him, sir. He's completely deluded. Your boon from the Sun is more powerful. You cannot compare the curse of a man, however powerful, to the boon of the Sun."

"Ha!" yelled the wild man. "Durvasa prevails!"

"No, he does not—the Sun does!"

Kundadanta was confused and alarmed. He bowed before the holy man and begged him to settle the dispute. The man smiled and answered briefly, "Consider which one of the two possesses inner truth. They can tell you that, right gentlemen?"

The pleasant companion nodded vigorously. "Yes, that is completely true. The boons depend on a pure and virtuous consciousness while the curse does not. When someone gets a boon from a god or a man, both parties—giver and receiver—are conscious of the fact. The giver is conscious of the receiver, and the receiver is conscious of the giver. The boon is the very essence of virtue—it does not require a body and can exist in the soul of a man. But when one is cursed, the curse has no such subtle existence, because the receiver denies it. It is not part of his essence." He looked at his companion triumphantly, while the latter lowered his eyes.

Kundadanta looked at the holy man and asked, "Does that mean that my boons will overcome the curses? Am I saved?"

The old man looked at him sadly for a few moments and responded, "Your boon may be satisfied, but trust me, you will not be. Look," he added after another pause, "it's rarely easy to tell the difference anyway. The boons and the curses usually coexist, and you end up with mixed results. You prefer the boon over the curse, but the result is that you see things as in a dream. Even being a ruler of the world is just the appearance of a boon."

"I don't follow you, sir. Do you mean to say that I will be ruler of the world, or not?"

The holy man smiled. "Can you not see the truth? It is right there in front of you. Have you never wondered how eight men can each be ruler of the entire world? Or how you can rule the world and still remain in your own house? You have done severe penance for twelve years, but you do not see through these paradoxes?"

Kundadanta merely shook his head silently.

"Listen, young man," the saint continued. "The boon seems superior to you and more real only because you want it. But it is inseparable from the curse, which you hate. The two must always travel together. Now look at your friends." The holy man picked up a stone and threw it at the vicious companion. The stone sailed through him as though he were made of smoke. Another stone then went flying and sliced through the foglike substance of the pleasant companion. "You see, they do not really exist. You made them up. They are figments of your limited consciousness."

"But where did they come from? They came to me, after all, when I was hanging in the tree . . . And why are they so odd-looking?" asked Kundadanta.

The holy man was calm. "They are your boon and your curse. They came to you as soon as you died."

"Died? What do you mean died?" Kundadanta was patting his chest and pinching his shoulders. He felt normal.

"Look at this," answered the holy man, picking up another rock. He threw it, and Kundadanta felt a soft swoosh as it sailed through his midsection. "The only way for you to obtain both your boon and your curse was to die. The moment you died on the tree both arrived."

These words were followed by a long silence. Kundadanta sat there, contemplating everything that had happened, and everything he knew. He did not feel as he had always believed death would feel. Mostly, he was confused and lonely. Then he asked, "So the answer to the paradoxes—how I can rule when my brothers rule and how I can rule from home—the answer is that I must die?"

"No, my dear. Death is no solution. Death only answers the paradox in one way. Your body dies so your spirit rules, and so forth. That's shallow. No, the positive solution is to realize that you brought your two companions into being through your own efforts. You must realize that your consciousness created them: home and world, one and many, good and bad. What is truly real, my friend, is void. Infinite consciousness is void. When you obtain that knowledge, you will see that you never left home, that you were always ruler of the whole world, that this desert is a lush forest, that the forest was always a desert. You are not yet ready, boy."

"How will I know when I am, sir?"

"Turn around, boy, and look at your companions now!"

Kundadanta turned around quickly, but the two were gone. In their place he saw his seven brothers, smiling, with their wives at their side. It was impossible to say whether they were alive or dead, whether they had been there all along, or not. He felt a loss of bearing, as though he had no place to stand. Then he heard the holy man.

"Just be patient, my boy. Take your time, and keep the right course. Eventually you will know."

I stood still, quietly gathering my thoughts. The story was not about moksha, or spiritual liberation, and I could not understand why he told it just then. I wanted to ask him, but the old man had moved ahead very rapidly and disappeared behind the banyan tree. How did he manage to move so fast? By the time I reached the bend in the path, walking past the scrubby bushes, it felt as though I had not seen him in eons. I turned the corner, and the old man was now seated on the ground, perfectly still, as though he had been here in meditation since the rocks formed. Behind him and up the mountain the terrain had changed drastically from the trees and scrub below. There was no vegetation at all, just a vast bowl-shaped plateau of rocks and boulders, the steely brown of volcanic basalt under the gray, cloudy sky. From his spot in front of a rock, the old guide calmly watched me approaching.

"Sir," I said, feeling a strange reverence that had not been there earlier, "can you finally clear my confusion? Would you please teach me the truth?" That was not quite what I had intended to ask; it came out sounding so grand, but an earnest feeling followed the words.

He looked at me seriously and gestured for me to sit down in front of him. I approached but remained standing. "What is the truth, sir?"

"Sit down."

His response sounded too mundane, so out of proportion with the gravity of the moment. It felt like a distraction, a delay. "Please just tell me what it is!"

"Sit down," he whispered.

I bent over then, partially facing him, and sat down.

The minute I came to rest on the ground, I realized the truth. My inner thoughts and great expectations evaporated, and I emptied out. The field of rocks suddenly crystallized into a vivid, eloquent image of merely what it was—an empty field of rocks. It was filled with a soft but clear light that emanated from the ground and the rocks. I felt the slow descent of relief and a surge of joy that completely defied pleasure. As I dissolved before every minute detail of every little stone, my consciousness at the same time expanded to embrace the entire mountainside.

"That's all there is!" What an astounding, simple fact. "That's all there is!"

I did not experience a fullness of Being, there was no Divine Presence, no grace. Instead, everything was completely empty of anything other than what it simply was. But at the same time everything was perfectly full. "All just is—supreme suchness, nothing more, nothing less. Bliss."

Every notion I had ever entertained about moksha and nirvana, about discipline and salvation, absented itself. There were no hopes or plans, no worrying or fearing. It had always been there, simple—not majestic—just the way it filled all of space, which was perfect. I turned my head toward the old man, whose features disappeared into the landscape around him. Then I realized that he was blurry because of the tears in my eyes. It was cold. I put on my shoes and stood up. The steps up the mountain were behind me, leading toward the west.

"Listen," he whispered, although I heard every syllable. "This is high enough for today. Don't go any farther." I turned again to look at the steps, and he continued, "Going farther will do you no good right now."

"But I'm so close to the top! And Shiva's huge bull is just around the corner ..."

"That makes no difference. It's better that you turn back now—in fact I want you to run down the mountain. Don't walk." I kneeled down next to the old man, who was now in deep trance. "Why do you want me to run? That makes no sense."

"Go!"

Before the word stopped booming around me, I was already down several steps. It was as though those first few steps never existed, as if I had been blown by a powerful percussion. Then I found myself hurtling down the mountain at a ridiculous speed, eyes glued to every step that rushed at me. The steps were uneven in height and depth, some were slippery and others were jagged, and I had a tiny fraction of a second to decide which was coming up next. I accelerated, leaned forward into a near stumble, no longer sure what kept me going. I felt the old man's eyes, but what could he do? Clutching the cane more firmly, I increased my speed. As I watched the shifting pattern of steps, always looking two ahead of my landing feet, the vegetation of the mountain became a green blur framing my field of vision. I gave myself over to the force that pushed—or was it pulling?—me down the mountain and suddenly realized something strange.

Because I was looking ahead of where my feet landed, something else must have been guiding them to the right spot! The perfect placement of each of my steps had nothing to do with planning or intention, or even the fear of falling.

Cheetahs don't have to plan their cuts, and impalas don't have to design their landings! The biologist in me screamed, "It's natural, you fool! Let go!" But that thought flashed and disappeared in the space of two steps. In its place I was back on the roof in Pune, realizing that mind was just riding piggyback on something else; it doesn't have to be in control because it isn't in control. At that very instant the steps disappeared. I kept going down, furiously, faster than ever, but the steps were gone, and my mind stopped scripting everything. Then the agent dissolved and running just happened on the northern slope of Chamundi Hill as the young biologist finally gave himself a break and let go, like a tired passenger leaning into his seat on a streaking train.

Strangely, all the motion now was taking place around me, and it was all uphill. The green blur of the landscape resolved into individual bushes, trees, and boulders; everything on the northern face of the hill was frantically running upward. "Hey, what's up there? Why are they running up?" Then I remembered—"Shiva! Shiva's up there, and they're all running up to be with Shiva." That made me laugh. Nims, tamarinds, banyans, and a myriad of bushes were jostling past me to get to him. What a riot. Faster and faster, everything moved in Shiva's direction, a parade, a race, a great stream of beings crushing up the mountain to God. Then the stories with their characters passed by: the weaver and his friend, Sangayya floated by with his eyes wide open in amazement, the women with their suitors, snakes, demons, sorcerers, thieves—all rushing up leaving a trail of cool microclimates in and out of which I sprinted.

Suddenly I could see the bottom of the mountain, the ground was starting to rush at me, and at the foot of the path was a tiny figure, a man. It was Rony, and he was waving something in the air in my direction—a postcard. Then I got to him and stopped.

"There you are! It's a card from your mother! You got a note from your mother, you lucky devil!" I couldn't speak. I just stood there, leaning on my knees and panting, watching my feet reattach themselves to my legs. "Hey, as you were whiling away the whole day on the mountain, I've been busy, pal. I went back to the hotel and got you some fruit, and there was this postcard for you. How did you like the old man with the stories?"

I bolted upright. "What did you say?"

"I said, how did you like the old man with the stories?"

"No, not that. What did you say before that, about the day on the mountain?"

"You mean 'as you were whiling away the whole day on the mountain'?"

"Yes! That's it!

"Well, that's what I said. What about it?"

Suddenly I understood the meaning of the last story, and all of them. I saw the meaning of the entire journey I had been through with the guide! That phrase my best friend had used—those innocuous, slightly judgmental words—that was one of my mother's favorite phrases. Every time she used it, I would cringe. I took the card from Rony's hand and looked at it. It featured one of those brilliant sunrises over the Sonora Desert—a standard Tucson postcard. On the back my mother wrote in her small and neat handwriting:

Hi Honey–
The monsoons were great this year–the desert flowers are gorgeous and they miss you. Enjoy India!
Love, Mom and Dad

That was it. Laconic and loving, no sentimental gushing. I missed her suddenly, as if I had not seen her in half a decade. I looked at Rony now, and he was watching me the way the guide might have.

"I get it now!" I said to him. "The last story—the whole trip. Listen, you and my mother are the companions from the last story—I made you up. I don't mean that I invented you, but in a sense maybe even that's true. You were the good one, the one who said all the right things and carried me forward. She was the bad one, the one who held me back, criticizing and judging. Just like the two companions in the story. But that split was just my imagination—there's no real difference. You're no better for my back, and she's no worse for my spirit. That was the work of mind."

Rony looked at me quietly. He seemed content to listen as I told him that the old man guided me—reluctant as I was—on a spiritual pilgrimage. Eventually I began to think that the goal was at the top of the mountain—God or moksha. Finally I geared up for some great revelation at the top. But when the old man felt I had made just enough progress, heard the right stories, he needed to show me that the goal was not at the top, but where I had started, down below. If the pilgrimage was to mean anything at all, it would have to lead toward my life, not away from it. The old man had been telling me that all along, in a hundred little ways. That's why he said the solar-love flower was my key: it links the solar messenger in the last story to my hospital days on the rack—the moment I began awakening. He ended his storytelling with the tale that would close the circle, end the narrative of the pilgrimage, and take me back to my reality—where I had two companions whom I had created, perhaps when I was hanging on my trees: the tree in Bath

County and the hospital device in Staunton. That's when my splitting of reality became obvious and should have dawned on me, and that is where the guide was leading me at the end.

I threw my head back and laughed. My legs quivered from lactic-acid buildup, and Rony laughed with me. "So, how many times have you been up this mountain anyway?" I asked him.

"Just enough to tell him all about you," answered my friend.

"And where do we go now?"

"There is only one place we can go."

I looked again at the postcard of the sun rising over the Sonora Desert, and nodded.